Becoming American?

Becoming American?

The Forging of Arab and Muslim Identity in Pluralist America

Yvonne Yazbeck Haddad

BAYLOR UNIVERSITY PRESS

Cover design by the BookDesigners

Library of Congress Cataloging-in-Publication Data

Haddad, Yvonne Yazbeck, 1935-
  Becoming American? : the forging of Arab and Muslim identity in pluralist America / Yvonne Yazbeck Haddad.
    p. cm.
  Includes bibliographical references.
  ISBN 978-1-60258-406-8 (hardback : alk. paper)
  1. Arab Americans--Ethnic identity. 2. Muslims--United States--Ethnic identity. I. Title.
  E184.A65H325 2011
  305.892'7073--dc23
                                        2011022342

Printed in the United States of America on acid-free paper with a 30% pcw recycled content.

Contents

◉

v

1

The Shaping of Arab and Muslim
Identity in the United States

◉

The al-Qaeda attacks of September 11, 2001, on the World Trade Center and the Pentagon are repeatedly depicted as having "changed America forever." Whether or not such hyperbole is completely justified, there can be little doubt of the reverberations of the event in all spheres of American life in general and in the lives of Muslims and Arabs living in the United States in particular. The questions that future scholars will have to investigate include whether the attacks had a lasting effect on Arabs and Muslims and their integration and assimilation in the United States, as well as what permanent impact, if any, they will have on the unfolding of the articulation of Islam in the American public square. Certainly the U.S. government is currently attempting to play an important role in such a reformulation of Islam through its high-intensity attempts to identify, one might even say create, a "moderate Islam," one that is definitively different from that espoused by those who perpetrated the attacks and justified their actions by reference to the religion of Islam.

There are no accurate figures for the number of Muslims in the United States. Neither the census data nor the records of the Immigration and Naturalization Service (INS) provide any information on religious affiliation of citizens or immigrants. Consequently, there exists a great disparity in the estimates of their number in the United States, from two million, as reported by B'nai Brith, to as many as eleven million, as reported by Warith Deen Mohammed, leader of the Muslim American Society (MAS), the largest African-American Muslim organization. The Council on American-Islamic Relations (CAIR), in all of its communiqués, gives the figure as seven million Muslims. While the numbers are contested, it is generally agreed that they are significant. The larger the community, Muslims believe, the bigger its potential impact in the political arena and influence on policy. The figures appear to be of similar importance to some in the Jewish community, who over a decade ago began warning about the "imminent threat" of a Muslim presence in America.[1]

An estimated three million Arabic-speaking people (and their descendants, a few of whom are in their sixth generation) now live in the United States, constituting about 1 percent of the population. The majority arrived during the last third of the twentieth century. The community is still in the process of being formed and re-formed as the policies of the American government regulate the flow of immigrants from the Arab world. Legislation limiting immigration, as well as American foreign policy and the prevailing American prejudice against Arabs, Muslims, and Islam, has at times accelerated and at other times impeded the integration and assimilation of the community into American society.

The Arab community in the United States is noted for its diversity, which is evident in its ethnic, racial, linguistic, religious, sectarian, tribal, and national identities. Today Arab-Americans are dispersed throughout the United States. Two-thirds of them live in ten states, including one-third in California, New York, and Michigan. About half of them (48 percent) live in twenty large metropolitan areas, with the highest concentrations in Los Angeles, Detroit, New York, Chicago, and Washington, D.C. About a quarter of them (23 percent) are Muslims (Sunni, Shi'ites, and Druze) and constitute a minority within the

Arab-American community, the majority of whom are Christian,[2] with a small Jewish minority.[3] Arab-Americans are also a minority (25 percent) within the Muslim-American community, which includes an estimated 33 percent South Asians and 30 percent African-Americans.[4]

The Arabic-Speaking Immigrants of the United States

A few Muslim males from the Syrian Province of the Ottoman Empire (today's Syria, Lebanon, Jordan, and Palestine/Israel) began arriving in the United States in the 1870s. They were rural migrant laborers hoping to make money and return to live in their homelands.[5] Their success, the deteriorating economy in the Middle East, and the subsequent famine precipitated by World War I brought about 4,300 additional Muslims to the United States between 1899 and 1914.[6] The flow of immigration was interrupted during World War I, and was curtailed by the National Origin Act of 1924, which restricted the number of immigrants from the Middle East to one hundred persons per year.

The early immigrants were classified by the officials of the INS as coming from "Turkey in Asia." These immigrants resented the Turkish designation, since many were running away from Ottoman conscription and oppression, as well as the Asia designation, since it excluded them from becoming citizens. By 1899 the INS began to add the subcategory of "Syrians" to their registration.[7] That became the identity of choice, as argued by Philip Hitti in *The Syrians in America*,[8] who insisted that Syrians were distinct from the Turks and had made great contributions to human civilization. They spoke of themselves as "wlad 'Arab" (children of Arabs), a reference to the language they spoke.

The early Muslim immigrants to the United States from Greater Syria were few in number. They came to the United States when racism and nativism were paramount, when "Anglo conformity" was promoted as the norm for citizenship and the Protestant establishment determined what was American. Like the millions of immigrants who passed through Ellis Island, they followed the patterns of integration and assimilation that refashioned them into American citizens. Their names were anglicized: Muhammad became Mo, Rashid became Dick, Mojahid became Mark, and Ali became Al. They dug ditches, laid railroad tracks, peddled, and later opened grocery stores and other businesses that catered to ethnic needs. Their children went to public schools and worked in factories. They enlisted in the American military during the First and Second World Wars and served with distinction.

The second wave of immigrants came after the end of World War II, when the United States assumed responsibility for the security of the oil fields in the Middle East and recruited students from the newly independent Arab states to study at American universities, with the expectation that once they returned to their home countries they would constitute an important asset to U.S. interests. They were predominantly of middle- and upper-class urban backgrounds and had the intimate experience of living in pluralistic settings. A large number were graduates of foreign educational institutions run by secular and missionary groups in the Arab world. Their instruction had been primarily in foreign languages and in Western curricula: American, British, French, German, and Russian. Two-thirds of the students married American wives. A large number of them decided to settle in the United States. By 1961, when Abdo A. Elkholy published his study on Arab-Muslims in Detroit, Michigan, and Toledo, Ohio, he estimated that the total number of Muslims of Arab origin in the United States was seventy-eight thousand, the majority of whom were from Lebanon. The other estimated thirty thousand were from Eastern Europe (Albania and Yugoslavia), Pakistan, and Turkey, with a few Tatars from the Soviet Union.[9]

The revocation of the Asia Exclusion Act in 1965 dramatically altered the constituency of the Muslim population of the United States. It brought immigrants from all areas of the Arab and Muslim world. The new immigrants were more representative of the ethnic, national, and religious diversity of the Muslim world. They included a large number of highly educated, socially mobile, professional Muslims—part of the Arab and South Asian "brain drain"—and more women. Meanwhile, the opening of the doors of emigration, the changes in immigration laws, and the lottery system, which gave visas to winners from all over the world, brought a different "kind" of immigrant. All social and economic classes from villages, towns, and cities stretching from Morocco to Yemen were represented. The majority of new Muslim immigrants came from the Indian subcontinent: India, Pakistan, and Bangladesh. The latest arrivals included a substantial number of refugees from countries racked by civil wars and often suffering the results of Western exploitation. Some have called them the "collateral damage" of American foreign policy in such countries as Algeria, Iraq, Lebanon, Somalia, and Palestine. Among them were some of the poorest of the dispossessed, with little or no formal education. They have been more concerned about survival than issues of identity and assimilation. Along with the refugees were those seeking political asylum from Algeria, Libya, Tunisia, and other autocratic regimes.

The "Arab" Muslims of the United States reflect the religious and sectarian divisions of the population of the Arab world. The largest group is Sunni. The percentage of the Shi'ite population in the United States is presumed to be larger than what obtains in the Arab world, due to the fact that their areas of residence were devastated by war (especially southern Iraq and Lebanon). The Shi'ites include Ithna 'Asharis (or Ja'faris) from Iraq, Lebanon, and Syria; Isma'ilis from Syria; Zaidis from Yemen; 'Alawis from Lebanon and Syria; and Druze from Israel, Lebanon, Palestine, and Syria. All of these groups have established their distinctive community organizations in the United States. They generally affirm that there are no differences between Shi'ites and Sunnis. But while they may worship in the same mosques, there have been incidents of tension over whether members of the two communities can intermarry, or whether one group can perform the burial prayer over a deceased person from the other.

Immigrants from the Arab world reflect also the variety of minority and ethnic communities that constitute the populations of these nations, including Armenians, Assyrians, Chechens, Circassians, Kurds, and Turcomans, who have been subjected to the Arabization programs of Arab governments since their independence. Many in these groups tend to dissociate themselves from Arab identity once they emigrate. Some do identify as Arabs or as Arab-Americans, while others have set up lobbies in Washington, collaborating with pro-Israeli groups, and engaging in defaming Arab nations. The Arabic language may seem to be the strongest common bond among Arabs and an initial indicator of ethnic identity. However, the variety of dialects makes it difficult, for example, for Maghrebis (North Africans) and Mashreqis (from the Levant and the Arabian Peninsula) to communicate. For most the common language is English.

Those who emigrated in the second half of the twentieth century brought with them diverse national identities, developed by the nation-state to inspire their loyal citizens so they would defend national security against outside enemies. For immigrants, their attachments to these national identities are continually tested by events in their home countries and by American foreign policy toward their countries. Such home ties became strained during the Gulf War in 1990–1991, when Gulf Arabs questioned the authenticity of the "Arabness" of citizens of the northern states (Egypt, Jordan, Morocco, Palestine, Syria, and Tunisia) who opposed Saudi Arabian and American retribution against Saddam Hussein, and dismissed them as "Arabized" peoples who did not understand the threat that Saddam's military posed to the Gulf states. At the same time, some Arabs of the northern tier criticized Gulf Arabs as greedy and gullible and accused them of contributing to the disempowerment of the Arab people in their willingness to spend tens of billions of dollars to support American destruction of Iraq and to empower Israel in the process.

Not all Arabs living in the United States are immigrants. Temporary residents appear to have some influence on immigrants, as they interact with them in cultural, social, religious, and political affairs. They include migrant laborers who come from different countries, with the largest number from Yemen.[10] Émigrés, as well as political and religious refugees, have some impact on the assimilation of the Arab immigrants, as they focus on events overseas. They live in limbo, awaiting a change in the political circumstances in their home countries. A third group is the thousands of students attending various colleges and universities throughout the United States. Other temporary residents include tourists, businesspeople, and relatives. They also include a large contingent of diplomats to the United States and the United Nations from fifty-seven Islamic nations, who continue to be active in Arab and Islamic affairs.

Two international Islamic organizations, the Muslim World League (MWL) and the Organization of the Islamic Conference (OIC), are recognized by the United Nations as nongovernmental organizations and have diplomats in New York City. The MWL had extensive involvement with Muslim organizations in the United States in the 1980s. It organized the Council of Masajid (places of worship) in North America, provided imams from overseas for the leadership of twenty-six mosques, and funded Islamic activity in the United States. Several other Arab nations, including Egypt, Iraq, Libya, Kuwait, Qatar, and the United Arab Emirates, have funded publications and construction of mosques, among other projects.

Becoming American

There are very few studies that document the Americanization of Arab-Muslims in the United States. In the late 1950s, Abdo Elkholy attempted to assess the acculturation and assimilation of two Muslim communities after the incubation period of at least a quarter century when immigrants from the Middle East lived in isolation. The immigration quota system of the 1920s, the Depression of the 1930s, and World War II limited communications and further immigration from the region. Elkholy focused his investigation on whether "adherence to the old religion which differs from the religion prevailing in the adopted culture," and particularly Islam, is an impediment to the assimilation of immigrants of Arab ancestry into the United States. His research demonstrated the invalidity of the theory that religion delays the assimilation of immigrant groups into the new culture. Focusing on the two Arab-American Muslim communities (some of whom were fourth generation) living in Toledo, Ohio, and Detroit, Michigan, he concluded that, although the two communities were formed by immigrants arriving at the same time from the same area in Lebanon and were identical ethnically and religiously, the Toledo community was both more assimilated and more religious.[11]

Elkholy determined that the factor appearing to have the most impact on Arab-Muslims' assimilation was their occupation. The Detroit community was predominantly working class, lived in a ghetto-like environment, maintained traditional perceptions of the family, perpetuated sectarian conflicts, and had virtually no interaction with non-Muslims.[12] In contrast, Elkholy described the Toledo Muslims as liberal, "Americanized by liquor." The members of the Toledo community had higher incomes, largely a result of their engagement in the liquor industry and ownership of 30 percent of the city's bars.[13] Aware that Islam forbids alcohol, they did not consume alcohol themselves, but rationalized selling it.[14] Although they had lived in disparate areas of the United States before settling in Toledo, they were generally related to one another, displayed a greater harmony between the generations, and appeared to share a common goal of preserving their middle-class social status. Although they attended mosque services, they appeared ignorant of important Islamic prescriptions. For example, they prayed on Sunday in the mosques without performing the required ablutions. They also maintained social relations with Christians, attended social events in churches, and displayed an American flag in the mosque.[15] Generally ignorant of Islamic prescriptions and ritual, the young members of the Toledo mosque used the building primarily as a social center. "The mosque had thus become not only the place for worship and religious instruction but also the popular place for the youth where American social activities range from dating to mixed dancing." (Of the young people in the survey, 82 percent did not know that ablutions were prescribed after sex.[16]) Elkholy also noted that "the same loudspeaker which broadcasts the recorded Qur'anic verses before Friday prayer now broadcasts the rock and roll music of the third generation and waltzes for the second."[17]

In Detroit, young Muslims were living through an economic recession. Elkholy disapproved of their leisure activities (their preferred music for dancing was the Lebanese *dabkeh*[18]) and described them as "scores of idle, jobless young men" who spent their time gambling and in fighting between cliques. They were, he went on, engaged in "night life activities to the Moslem 'beat' generation" and were "religiously weak." He attributed their behaviors to authoritarian parents and saw the mosque as a place for "men" who were "aged and backward."[19]

Elkholy also noted that factors leading other immigrants to assimilate in the United States, such as language acquisition and preference for middle-class areas of residence, were also molding Arab-Muslims into American citizens. He argued that Islam was functioning as an assimilating religion by bringing the communities together as they began to shed their ethnic identities. In fact, he observed that the third generation in Toledo was more religious, while that of Detroit was more nationalistic, and that strong religious affiliation in the Toledo community accelerated, rather than hindered, its assimilation.[20]

A quarter century after Elkholy's study, another study of five Muslim communities, published in 1985, found that acculturation and assimilation were progressing among Muslims despite the influx of a large number of new immigrants from different areas with distinctive identities.[21] The study focused on five groups of Muslim settlers in the United States, four of which had established mosques by the 1930s (Dearborn, Michigan; Toledo, Ohio; Cedar Rapids, Iowa; and Quincy, Massachusetts) and another, made up primarily of Pakistani immigrants, that had established a new mosque in Rochester, New York. The 1985 survey noted that the traditional role of the imam had been transformed, even though a few of the imams, supported by the Muslim World League, had attempted to replicate the tradition of authority that obtained overseas. In several instances, the imams were overruled by their congregations, who had invested the decision-making role in the mosques' elected executive committees. From being a leader of prayer, the imam in the United States had taken on the role of a pastor, providing counseling and instruction in the faith, representing the community to the general public, participating in interfaith activities, and defending the faith.

The 1985 survey found that over two-thirds of the Muslims sampled had graduate degrees, making this the best-educated Muslim population in the world. Their educational achievement was also well above the national average of the United States. While it is possible that only the highly educated chose to participate in the study, further research revealed that these immigrants placed great stress on college education as a means of social and economic mobility. One Arab-American in her sixties who grew up in Ohio reported proudly, "My parents came to this country as illegal immigrants. They were both illiterate, but they worked hard and put all eight children through college."

The immigrant cohort of the fifties came to the United States for higher education, and, as American higher education expanded in the 1960s, a great number became professors at universities. While a significant number of this group became professionals and businesspeople in the United States, it was mostly the immigrants who were admitted on preference visas after 1965 who became doctors and engineers. They brought with them a special enthusiasm for these two professions, which are highly prized in the Arab world as a means to social and economic mobility. Many parents pressured their sons to follow in their footsteps. In the middle of the 1990s, the children of this group began to specialize in law, journalism, and the social sciences.

Further trends in Americanization, as noted by Elkholy, included the adoption of values that are contrary to Arab customs, particularly in choosing a marriage partner. Whereas arranged marriages are still in effect in large parts of the Arab world, the Arab-Muslim communities of Detroit and Toledo considered marriage to be a matter of personal choice, with courtship emulating American patterns. But the majority (71 percent) had married Muslims. Although about half the communities (45 percent in

Toledo, 45 percent in Detroit) opposed the marriage of females to non-Muslims, Elkholy also found that two-thirds of the people interviewed would not oppose interfaith marriages if the spouses were allowed to practice their faiths.[22] More recently, while arranged marriages have continued to be the norm among the majority of the children of recently arrived immigrants, especially those from small towns and rural areas, new means of matchmaking have been devised, including advertising in ethnic and religious magazines and through an Internet service. On college campuses, many young Arab-Americans have become indistinguishable from their colleagues in that they go to bars, date, drink, and smoke pot.

Elkholy concluded that Muslim women increased their participation in public life as part of their Americanization. He reported that "the family pattern of these two communities is approximately American. The wife is not merely the equal of her husband; she also dominates the family." Although he noted that wives help their husband in their business ventures, he failed to realize that, in the rural areas of Lebanon, from which these immigrants had come, women had previously played an important part in economic and public life.

The later research survey uncovered an important fact in Dearborn: that women were the primary instigators in establishing the mosque. They not only took the initiative in securing a place for the religious and social activities of the community, but they also raised the funds necessary, through bake sales and door-to-door soliciting. They managed the activities in the mosque facilities, arranging for weddings, receptions, and *haflehs* that included dancing. The influx of new immigrants into Dearborn, primarily Yemeni male migrant laborers, with a different cultural understanding of the role of women in society created a crisis in the community. The Yemenis, who seized control of the mosque through the courts by arguing that its extrareligious activities were un-Islamic, dispatched the women to the basement, and restricted their access to the mosque through a separate door. Thus, the new immigrants attempted to recreate their notion of Muslim society in the American context. Other actors, primarily the recently imported foreign imams who were hired to run the mosques, attempted to enforce gender segregation. Scandalized by the dancing and social events taking place in the mosques, they insisted that they be used exclusively for prayer and religious instruction.

The majority of the Muslim women in the United States during the 1960s did not veil. Veiling was generally perceived to be part of the maintenance of old customs, which were already dying out in Middle Eastern urban areas.[23] The 1985 study corroborated Elkholy's findings of Americanization.[24] It found that the degree of strictness in adhering to "Islamic dress" varied from one mosque to another. Some mosques permitted women to attend prayer in knee-length skirts and no head coverings, whereas others insisted that women cover all their bodies and in some cases provided them with wraps.[25] The more recent arrival of new immigrants who believed that the covering of the woman's hair is a divine commandment has led to an increase in the number of women voluntarily donning the *hijab*, even though, in many cases, their mothers had never worn one and their grandmothers had cast it away in the 1920s and 1930s. Also recently affecting the role of women is the immigration of Muslims from South Asia who advocate more traditional customs, including even the banning of handshaking between the sexes.[26]

Islamic knowledge continued to be restricted to male expertise. Women's religious activity was mostly restricted to "sisters" groups. Although women did lead study circles that focused on Islamic knowledge and the teachings of the Qur'an, these were generally conducted in private homes. By the 1990s, some Muslim women had begun to make their contributions to public life as academics, teachers, and researchers. Some were working through the Islamic historical and juridical sciences to reinterpret and provide new insights into Islamic knowledge and had published many studies on the role and status of women in Islam. In an effort to influence the cultural and social restrictions on women, some have offered new progressive insights and interpretations grounded in the text of the Qur'an and the example of the Prophet Muhammad.

In the United States, mosque attendance is a family affair rather than a strictly male activity, as in Muslim countries. Muslim women do attend *jum'a* (Friday communal prayers), albeit in smaller numbers than the Sunday family prayers. In some mosques, women's allotted space for prayer is located at the back of the prayer hall behind the men. At other mosques, women are at the side, often separated by a barrier or a curtain. Occasionally, women pray in a separate space, such as a basement, a loft, or an auxiliary room, where they can watch the service on closed-circuit television. Most women interviewed found the separation helped them to concentrate on prayer rather than on members of the opposite sex.

The "Arab" Experience of America

Who is an Arab? What is an Arab? How does one become an Arab? These questions were hotly debated in the formative period of the modern Arab nation-states during the first half of the twentieth century and continue to generate a great deal of discussion. An Arab nationalist identity was proposed as the foundation for a modern state that would consider as Arab all who speak the Arabic language and identify with Arab history and culture, regardless of whether they are Muslims, Christians, or Jews. This multireligious view was promoted primarily by Jews and Christians in an effort to carve out a national identity where religious minorities would be recognized as full citizens. It was also propagated by some Arabic-speaking Muslims opposing the Young Turks who were seeking to "Turkify" all ethnic and tribal groups resident in the Ottoman Empire. Today, several other meanings may be given to the word "Arab." One, for example, restricts the term to those who are native to the Arabian Peninsula as opposed to those who live in the "Arabized" northern tier (Iraq, Lebanon, Syria, Jordan, Palestine, Egypt, and North Africa). Another, much broader definition is based on citizenship in any of the twenty-two Arab states that are members of the Arab League.

Immigrants from the Arab world are, in a manner of speaking, veterans of the struggle to modernize and westernize in the context of the colonial and postcolonial era. They perceive the United States as a nation that has some very strong institutions, that sees itself as a model democracy, and that welcomes all who choose to share in the American dream. It seems to be a nation that advocates openness and pluralism as foundational principles of its polity. But somewhere behind these principles lurks the possibility of an anti-Saracen heritage that is as anti-Arab and anti- Muslim as it is anti-Semitic, if not more so.[27] Indeed, surveys of the media have documented the demonization of Arabs, Islam, and Muslims as the monolithic "outsiders," the essential "other," whose beliefs and customs are characterized as inferior, barbaric, sexist, and irrational—values worthy of repeated condemnation and eradication.[28]

Arab-American identity has been honed and reshaped by the immigrants themselves in response to American attitudes and policies toward them as well as their original homeland. This identity is also fashioned by the immigrants' local American experiences, the places in which they settle, their relations with older generations of immigrants, the reception and treatment they endure in their new environment, the diversity of the community with which they associate, their involvement in organized religion, and their attendance at ethnic or integrated mosques. Increasingly, it has also been profoundly influenced by American prejudice and hostility toward Arabs and Muslims, both real and perceived.

Arab-Americans have attempted to synthesize their experiences of America with the Arab and Muslim experience of a dominant "West" during the history of European colonial expansion and subjugation of the Muslim world beginning in the sixteenth century and lasting through the first half of the twentieth century. Western domination of Arab nations has been perceived as continuing through American hegemony and intervention in the area since the 1950s, and as manifest today in what Arabs see as the American support of Israeli colonial and expansionist policies in Palestine and the surrounding Arab states. American support for autocratic regimes that appear to be clients of American interests, and the recent American-declared war on terrorism, implemented through regime change in Afghanistan and Iraq and widely perceived by the Arab and Muslim world as a war on Islam, appear to fit the same pattern.

The Encounter with Zionism

The early immigrants from the Middle East were concerned about the fate of their relatives back home in the aftermath of World War I. A few lobbied the American government to help create the Arab state promised in the Faisal-McMahon Correspondence, and some Maronites worked for the creation of Greater Lebanon. However, the majority of immigrants did not appear to be interested in political activity. Rather, most of their early organizations were social, ethnic, or religious in nature.

The Syrian and Lebanese American Federation of the Eastern States was formed in Boston. Its membership included a variety of organizations, including social clubs, cultural groups, and charitable organizations. In 1932 the National Association of Syrian and Lebanese-American Organizations, later the National Association of Federations of Syrian and Lebanese-American Clubs (NAFALAC), was formed. In the early 1950s, the NAFALAC sponsored a convention in Lebanon to foster goodwill among the United States, Syria, and Lebanon. "During the life of the federation movement up until the 1960s, there was little real interest in the Middle East question by the majority of the member groups, although convention resolutions did often express feelings by the leadership that Zionism was a threat to Arab and American relations and was not in the best interest of the United States."[29] There is little evidence that the majority of the membership, a substantial number of whom were second and third generation, had any awareness of events overseas or the geography of the Middle East. Some of them had even contributed to the United Jewish Appeal. The NAFALAC ceased to exist in the late 1950s and early 1960s.

By the 1940s, the Arabic-speaking immigrants in the United States began to feel uncomfortable as the Zionist campaign for the recognition and support for the state of Israel became intense. Among the slogans adopted by the Zionists was "A land without a people for a people without a land."[30] The immigrants knew better. Not only was Palestine populated by Palestinians, both Christian and Muslim, but some of the immigrants still had relatives and friends in Haifa, Jaffa, Ramallah, Beit Jala, Jerusalem, the Galilee, and elsewhere. The most galling Zionist slogan, which had a far-reaching influence on Arabs, openly solicited funds for the eradication of Arabs: "Pay a dollar, kill an Arab." It had a great impact on Sayyid Qutb, an Egyptian author on a scholarship in the United States between 1949 and 1951. An agnostic, he returned home totally disillusioned with the United States, which he characterized as racist anti-Arab, anti-Muslim. Back in Egypt, he became active in the Muslim Brotherhood movement and became the greatest advocate of Islamism as an alternative to capitalism and communism, as a system that guaranteed justice and equality, where there is no distinction based on color or national identity.

By the 1950s, the impact of the conflict in the Middle East on the Muslim community in Detroit was palpable. Elkholy noted that they emphasized they were Arab, regardless of whether they had emigrated from Lebanon, Iraq, Syria, or Yemen.[31] One interviewee told Elkholy that "wherever a party is opened in the name of the Prophet, no one is particularly moved. If it is opened in the name of God, no one cares either. But the name of Gamal Abdel-Nasser electrifies the hall."[32] He attributed the phenomenon to the "continuing threat posed by the existence of Israel and Nasser's resistance to Israel and the Western political pressure."[33]

A substantial number of the new Muslim immigrants brought a different identity, one fashioned by the devastating experience of the Israeli attack of 1967 and the catastrophic Arab defeat (*al-Nakba*), the failed Arab counterattack in 1973, the Israeli invasion of Lebanon in 1982, and the massacres of Sabra and Shatila in 1983. The Lebanese civil war, in which the Maronite Christians colluded with Israel against the Palestinians, led to Muslim distrust of Arab Christians. The new immigrants represented a generation that had wearied of Arab nationalism, which they perceived to have failed to deliver on the hopes of Arab people for justice for the Palestinian people, for parity with the West, and for input into the world order. Their identity was shaped by the ideology that was beginning to sweep across the Arab world, one that affirmed religious identity as a means of resistance to fundamentalist secularism, promoted by a variety of regimes in the Middle East, as well as hegemonic "Judeo-Christianity," experienced as the "dominance of expansionist Israel as supported and empowered by Western nations." They had come to subscribe to some form of Islamic identity, and included a small minority who favored "Islamism" as the only way to foster unity and strength to combat what were perceived as incessant efforts to undermine Islam and Muslims.

Those who came in the 1980s had witnessed the Iranian revolution of 1979, which demonstrated the power of Islamic identity in mobilizing the population to dethrone the shah, "the mightiest of tyrants," who was considered a lackey of the United States and Israel. These experiences generated a growing consensus that Arab nationalist identity was a colonial construct devised to divide the Muslims and separate them into ethnic, racial, and language groups in order to dominate them. The new understanding was that only an Islamic identity, creating solidarity with other Muslim nations, can provide the necessary resources to fight for Muslim causes. The Arab states, went this line of thinking, would be empowered by the larger Muslim support from Indonesia, Pakistan, and elsewhere.

The prevailing American hostility toward Arabs during the 1967 Israeli preemptive strike against Egypt, Syria, and Jordan, and the immigrants' awareness of the ignorance of the American public about the facts of the conflict in the Middle East, led to the formation of the first organization to assume a hyphenated identity, coining the term "Arab-American." The Association of Arab-American University Graduates (AAUG) was formed in 1967 by graduate students, professionals, university professors, lawyers, doctors, and veterans of the Organization of Arab Students (OAS). It reflected an Arab nationalist ideology and made no distinction among members based on religious affiliation or national origin. It placed special emphasis on production of knowledge and the education of its membership, as well as the American public, about the Arab world.

They immediately became the target of the Zionist lobby, which began to portray Arab activists as spies and propagandists for foreign interests.[34] The *Near East Report* devoted several issues in 1969 to the "alleged threat" of the presence of Arabs in the United States. The expressed concern was over Arab "propaganda" on American campuses. To its editors, "the Arab viewpoint reaching American ears was of equal concern as alleged security threats."[35] They warned Americans that Arab students might harbor *fedayeen* among them and that Arabs were trying to infiltrate leftist organizations. Other lobby groups became active in silencing professors of Middle Eastern Studies on American campuses, asking for the elimination of funding for centers supported by Title VI to provide experts in area studies for government services. The lobby also targeted politicians who questioned American support of Israel, including Senator Percy of Illinois and Senator Fulbright of Arkansas, both of whom were perceived to have lost their elections because of the funding of their opponents from the Israeli lobby.[36]

Other Arab-American organizations were established by the second and third generations, veterans of the earlier federations. They were formed to defend the civil and political rights of the community and in response to American government policies that targeted Arab-Americans. Operation Boulder was launched in 1972 by the Nixon administration after the massacre of Israeli athletes at Munich. The United States government sought the help of the Israeli government and pro-Israeli organizations in the United States to spy on the community.[37] It shared intelligence with the Israeli government and appropriated the Israeli designation of "Arabs as terrorists."[38] The FBI began to compile dossiers on organizations and on members of the community by tapping their telephones and gathering information about their political ideas, the journals to which they subscribed, and their circle of friends.[39] Operation Boulder featured intimidation by FBI agents, the restriction of movement by Arabs in the United States, and the deportation of hundreds on technical irregularities. Immigration from the Arab world was restricted. Although Operation Boulder officially came to an end in 1975, harassment of politically active Arab-Americans continued, with the apparent purpose of intimidating the community and discouraging Arab political activity. This massive scrutiny did not result in identifying any anti-American activities.[40]

Other government actions and policies increased the marginalization of Arab-Americans and heightened their anxiety. Utilizing the Freedom of Information Act, the Arab community learned that in 1986 the American administration was considering the use of two military compounds in the South for the possible internment of Arabs and Iranians, as had been done to the Japanese during World War II. They were shocked by the way that anti-Arab perceptions were encouraged by the ABSCAM investigation,[41] when FBI agents masqueraded as Arabs in order to trap members of Congress. Such events, perceived as a vicious and racially discriminatory campaign against persons of Arab origin, offended the dignity of many Arab-Americans, particularly the American-born of Syrian and Lebanese origin who viewed themselves as loyal and law-abiding Americans and who had fought to defend the United States and its interests and values in World War I and World War II.[42] Second- and third-generation Lebanese-Americans organized the National Association of Arab Americans (NAAA) in 1972. Modeled after the pro-Israel lobby the American Israel Public Affairs Committee,[43] its leadership sought to educate Arab-Americans about the political process as well as arrange for them to meet with members of Congress to discuss issues of great concern to the community. In addition, the American-Arab Anti-Discrimination Committee (ADC) was founded by former American-born Senator James Aburezk and James Zogby, both of Christian Lebanese origin.[44] It was modeled after the ADL (Anti-Defamation League) to fight racism, prejudice, and discrimination against Arabs. It is currently the largest grassroots Arab organization, with chapters throughout the United States.

The Arab American Institute (AAI) was established in 1984 when James Zogby split from the ADC. It encourages Arab-Americans to participate in the American political system, working to get them to vote and to run for office. It has sought to establish Democratic and Republican clubs, such as those active in the presidential campaigns of Jesse Jackson (1988), Gore-Lieberman (2000), and Bush-Cheney (2000). Arab immigrants generally lack experience in political participation, fear the consequences of political involvement, and have no experience in coalition building. Major political candidates, including George McGovern, Walter Mondale, Joseph Kennedy, and Mayor Goode of Philadelphia, often out of fear of antagonizing the pro-Israel lobby, have shunned them and returned their financial contributions because they are perceived as a liability. In the 2000 New York senatorial contest, Republican candidate Rick Lazio depicted Arab and Muslim contributions to Hillary Clinton's campaign as "blood-money," which led to her returning the donations. Many in the community feel disenfranchised, given the importance of donations in providing access to elected officials and determining American policies.

All Arab-American organizations were formed by a coalition of Christians and Muslims from the Arab states. What held them together was the shared view of American stereotyping of Arabs and Muslims and their shared interpretations of events in the Middle East. The organizations were cemented by a perception of Zionist stalking of their activities and intimidation of their speakers, and by a deep commitment to the American democratic process. They expected America to live up to its proclaimed values and placed their trust in the American judicial system and the guarantees of the Constitution and Bill of Rights.

The Muslim Experience of America

Once the pioneer Muslim migrants from the Arab world decided to settle in the United States, they were eager to belong, and in the process they tried to interpret American culture as compatible with Arab concepts of virtue and honor. They emphasized the similarities between Islam and Christianity—for example, the respect Islam has for Jesus and his mother Mary. Early records show that they were dispersed throughout the United States and initially tended to socialize with Christian and Jewish immigrants from the Arab world. They sent their children to Christian parochial schools in order to imbue their education with ethical values. It was not until the 1930s that they began to have structures dedicated to Islamic services. In communicating with the American public, they tended to talk about the Qur'an as "our bible," the mosque as "our church," the imam as "our minister." Their great-grandchildren are now indistinguishable from other Americans. Their dispersion and isolation, as well as the hardships they went through, led to little organized activity. Some belonged to the Syrian and Lebanese Federations.

Abdullah Igram of Cedar Rapids, Iowa, a veteran of World War II who experienced marginalization in the American military, worked to bring Islam and its adherents into the mainstream by seeking recognition from President Eisenhower. He requested that the religious affiliation of Muslims be recognized by the U.S. military, which previously left it blank on their "dog tags." In 1953, he called for a general meeting of Muslims, and members from twenty-two different mosques and centers in the United States and Canada participated. The next year they formed the Federation of Islamic Associations in the United States and Canada (FIA), which eventually had a membership of fifty-four mosques and Islamic centers. Reflecting the constituency of the Muslim population in the United States in the 1950s, the majority of the congregations of these mosques were Lebanese.

The immigrants of the 1970s often found the accommodation of the earlier immigrants to American culture too high a price to pay, especially since America began to define itself as Protestant, Catholic, and Jewish. They found the social and spiritual problems of America repugnant, even as they enjoyed America's economic opportunities and freedom of religion, association, and speech. They accused the earlier immigrants of diluting the importance of Islamic traditions, rituals, and distinguishing characteristics. They believed that difference and distinctiveness were a necessary means of affirming a place for Islam. Their conscious religious observances and their publications emphasized the great importance of the manner of prayer and how women were to dress, walk and talk. Rather than stressing commonalities with American culture and religion, they emphasized the differences. They were confident that Islam is the perfect way and the cure for all that ails America.

Other factors contributed to the development of Islamic institutions in the United States in the 1990s. For one thing, there was a dramatic growth in the number of Muslim immigrants to the United States between 1970 and 1990, creating a larger cohort group of practicing Muslims. Many came from the middle and lower middle classes in rural areas and elected to maintain their traditional dress, while finding in mosque institutions a support system that helped them establish networks and find jobs and companionship.

The Salman Rushdie affair affirmed for Muslim observers the lack of Western sympathy for Islamic sensitivities. They noted that the media emphasized the condemnation of *The Satanic Verses* as a negation of freedom of speech in a country that believes that books should not be censored. However, they also could not help but see that the speech codes of the United States and political correctness have generally frowned on works of fiction that offend Jewish and African-American sensitivities, such as *The Protocols of the Elders of Zion* and *Little Black Sambo*. That the American establishment refused to condemn *The Satanic Verses* was seen as yet another example of demonizing Islam and Muslims. For many, it was a signal that they had not arrived as yet.

The last decade of the twentieth century ushered in a new phase in Muslim integration and assimilation into the United States. Several factors coalesced to bring about a major transformation in the Muslim community. The Gulf War of 1990 marked the end of financial support from Saudi Arabia and other

Gulf nations. Initially, the withdrawal of support had a devastating effect on Islamic projects in the United States. Both ISNA and FIA shut down for lack of funds to pay their staff. But communal paralysis did not set in. Several of the alumni of the Muslim Student Association welcomed the freedom from dependency and began to work to establish permanent Islamic institutions. In the process, the power shifted from umbrella organizations to decentralized leadership, the independent mosque executive committees. While ISNA reopened with a skeleton staff, its ability to control and guide the progress of Islam nationwide had been greatly diminished. Its journal, *Islamic Horizon*, continues to be distributed nationally, and its annual conventions draw about thirty thousand Muslims. It has recently started hosting annual academic conferences on "Islam in America," "Islam in Prisons," and "Islam among Latinos," which provide important insights on the daily life of Muslims in North America.

While the 1980s saw the development of Arab-American organizations interested in public policy, the 1990s saw the emergence of several Islamic organizations. The American Muslim Alliance (AMA) was formed in California in 1989 by Agha Saeed. Its goal was to empower Muslims to participate in the political process by voting and running for office. Others included the American Muslim Council (AMC, founded in 1990), the Council on American Islamic Relations (CAIR, 1994), and the Muslim Public Affairs Council (MPAC). Their goals generally paralleled those of the Arab organizations that came into existence in the 1980s, since several of the leaders were alumni of those organizations who saw a growing need to create Islamic institutions to engage the non-Arab Muslims in supporting a variety of political and civil rights issues relevant to the growing Muslim community.

With the election of Bill Clinton as president of the United States, Muslims perceived a major transformation in the political allegiances of government policy makers. Clinton was beholden to the Jewish community because of its extensive support during his campaign. At the urging of Senator Joseph Lieberman, Democrat of Connecticut, the new administration brought twenty-seven activists from the pro-Israeli lobby into the government and placed them in charge of Middle East policy. During his two terms in office, they were able to weave the U.S.-Israel relationship into a seamless entity. It appeared to Muslims and Arabs that American interests in the Middle East were being subsumed under the primary interests of Israel.

At the same time that the government's foreign policy initiatives were deemed anti-Palestinian and anti-Muslim, the Clinton administration initiated a policy of symbolic inclusion of American Muslims. Periodically, leaders of the various Muslim organizations were invited to public events and occasionally had an audience with policy makers and talked about their issues. Mrs. Clinton hosted the first *iftar* dinner (the break of the fast of Ramadan) at the Department of State. Although some in the Muslim leadership were enamored of what they perceived as elevation of their status, they were fully aware that while they could voice their concerns during these brief encounters, they had no influence on policy.

Confident in an American Muslim future, Muslims in various suburbs and cities stepped out of the shadows and became more visible. They turned to their own resources and began building mosques and Islamic centers, whose number grew from 598 in 1986 to over 1,250 by 2000. Some of the mosques built in the middle of the century were architecturally nondescript and were remodeled or replaced by new structures with minarets, cupolas, and domes, symbols of Islamic architecture. A few of the mosques started social and welfare organizations (such as soup kitchens and free medical clinics) to serve the needy in America, breaking the practices of earlier generations who sent their *zakat* funds to support the poor relatives and the dispossessed of the lands they left behind. Over two hundred Islamic schools were established. Islam was entering the mainstream, and the Muslim community had decided that it was in America to stay. It consciously began to put its imprint on the American landscape, a permanent settlement set in brick, concrete, tile, and stone.

Meanwhile, Arab-American identity had become associated with Christians and secular Muslims from the Arab world. There was a growing consensus among Islamists that Arab identity had been divisive and had led to the disempowerment of Arabs. From their perspective, anyone who identifies himself as Arab places national over religious identity. Increasingly, Muslim immigrants from Arab nation states identify themselves either as Muslim or by the citizenship they held prior to emigration: Egyptian, Palestinian, Syrian, and the like. Very rarely does an immigrant identify himself by saying, "I am an Arab Muslim," unless he is from the Gulf area or is trying to make a linguistic or geographical distinction. For many among the third-wave immigrants, "Arab" has become a secondary modifier of identity, which is in a state of flux depending on context. Their primary identity can be Shi'i, Muslim, Lebanese, Arab, or American, depending on the circumstances that demand differentiation.

Whereas early mosque activities centered on fostering a social community that shared a common faith, in the 1990s the mosque became a center for creating an Islamic ethnicity based not only on a shared faith, but also on a shared worldview that envisioned a Muslim community engaged with American society, taking its place in the American religious mosaic.

Claiming Muslim Space in America's Pluralism

Who is a Muslim? When does one cease to be a Muslim? What is the relation of Islam to culture, to politics, to economic practices, and how does a Muslim maintain adherence to Islamically prescribed and proscribed admonitions that relate to these issues? Given the broad range of backgrounds and associations, what practices and beliefs are negotiable, fixed, or malleable? How does the cultural baggage carried by the immigrants influence their perception of Islamic culture as it takes root in America? Is there a possibility of reinterpreting Islamic jurisprudence to provide more options for behavior in the American context? Does the slogan "Islam is valid for all times and places" necessitate consensus on a particular prototype that has to be implemented wherever Islam is transplanted, or is there room for reinterpretation to help Muslims adjust to the new environment in which they find themselves? Can Muslims tolerate the different choices that members in the community make, or should they deem those who veer from the proclaimed laws beyond the pale? Can a Muslim live in a non-Muslim environment and continue to be considered a believer? These and other questions have been the focus of extensive discussion and debate during the twentieth century.

The immigrants had no experience of being a minority, of living in diaspora, or of creating institutions or organizing religious communities. They had no imams or religious leaders to provide instruction in the foundations of the faith. In the nations they left behind, religious affairs were the domain of governments. They had to figure out whether their living in a non-Muslim state, or eating the meat sold in its stores owned by non-Muslims, was religiously sanctioned. They sought juridical justification for their choices and counsel on what institutional forms to create.

Islamic juridical opinion has addressed these issues in a variety of contexts throughout Islamic history. The legal opinion of the medieval jurists is often quoted to provide validation for modern interpretations. Given the wide range of opinions and the variety of contexts that they addressed over a span of fourteen centuries, it is not surprising that there is no absolute consensus on the issue.[45] In the contemporary era, the voluntary emigration of Muslims to non-Muslim nations has once again raised the issue of the legitimacy of residing in a non-Muslim environment.

The early immigrants had no Islamic leadership and no access to juridical opinion. They were aware of the *fatwas* of Muhammad Abduh, Shaykh al-Azhar of Egypt, permitting the consumption of meat slaughtered by People of the Book (Christians and Jews) as well as Muslim collaboration with non-Muslims for the benefit that accrued to the Muslim community.[46] They were also aware of the *fatwa* by Rashid Rida approving residence of Muslims in a non-Muslim environment. Quoting al-Mawardi, a famous medieval jurist, he reported that the Prophet did not proscribe residence in non-Muslim areas, but had actually allowed Muslims to do so if they were accorded the freedom to practice their faith.[47]

As noted earlier, the immigrants who came after the repeal of the Asia Exclusion Act included Muslims who had given up on the nationalist ideology and were influenced by the Islamic vision of a society that is an alternative to Marxism and capitalism, one that is eager to recreate an Islamic order in the world. Many were influenced by the writings of Mawlana Abu al-A'la al-Mawdudi, founder of the Jama'ati Islami of the subcontinent, and Sayyid Qutb, ideologue of the Muslim Brotherhood in Egypt.[48] Mawdudi's ideology was incubated in the struggle for the creation of an Islamic state in Pakistan, while Qutb's ideas were influenced by what he experienced as racism and his exposure to pro-Israeli, anti-Arab, anti-Muslim propaganda during his residence in the United States, as well as by his reactions to the socialist-secularist policies of Abdul Nasser. Both Mawdudi and Qutb advocated a sharp bifurcation between Islam and nationalism, between the Muslim *umma* and all other social and political systems, which they designated as *jahiliyya*, a reference to the polytheistic society that obtained in Arabia at the time of the revelation of the Qur'an. For both, the mission of Muslims in the world was to combat un-Islamic orders and not to compromise with them.

Qutb fashioned an ideology of resistance advocating the creation of a vanguard group who would refuse to live under regimes that persecuted Muslims for their beliefs or placed impediments in the way of creating an Islamic state. Mawdudi traveled extensively in the United States and Canada during the 1960s and 1970s warning the recently arrived Muslim immigrants about living in a non-Muslim environment. He later moderated his views and taught that residence in the United States provides the opportunity for delivering the saving message of Islam to America. Another influential Muslim speaker, Syed Abu al-Hassan Ali Nadvi of India, traveled extensively in the United States and Canada urging Muslims to maintain a separate community. He urged the immigrants to be steadfast in the faith. "You, therefore, are in America not merely as flesh and blood, not simply as Indians, Pakistanis, Egyptians, Syrians . . . but as Muslims, one community, one brotherhood. You are Ibrahimi and Muhammadi. Know yourself. You have not come here to lose your identity and get fitted into this monstrous machine or to fill your bellies like animals."[49] He warned against being blinded by the search for wealth and losing one's distinctive identity. "Should there be the least danger to faith go back to your native land or to any other place where there is the security of faith; go, and take your family, go even if you have to go on foot."[50]

Overseas, interest in the condition of vulnerable Muslim minorities in the world increased during the 1970s and 1980s. M. Ali Kettani, a North African, wrote a book on Muslim minorities, identifying "minorityness" as a condition of powerlessness of the community, regardless of its numerical strength. He feared that this condition might lead Muslims to compromise with those in power and acquiesce to their demands, restricting their freedom to practice the faith. If that occurs, it becomes their incumbent Islamic duty to try to alter their situation. If they are unable to change their circumstances, they have to emigrate to a more congenial environment where they can practice their faith without impediment, or they have to organize and fight back against their oppressors. To emigrate is to emulate the example of the Prophet in search of freedom to practice the faith. It has a profound religious significance, since in this act they are not accommodating oppressive power but continuing to work for the establishment of a just society. This emigration has two possible goals: one seeks the return to the place of origin in order to restore it to the true faith; the other is to establish a permanent settlement in an effort to create a new Islamic society. Kettani recommended that immigrant Muslims create residential enclaves and local institutions that support the building of an Islamic community without divisions according to national origin, class, sectarian, or partisan affiliation. The goal is to protect the community from assimilation into the new environment that would lead to its disintegration. It must guard its distinctiveness and maintain Islamic cultural markers. He urged the Muslim community to take control of the education of their children, to emphasize the use of the Arabic language, wear Islamic dress, and assume Islamic names. From his perspective, the enclave is not a ghetto, but rather a model Muslim community that fosters and promotes the realization of Islamic principles in daily life, hence becoming a witness to the greater society.[51]

The 1980s brought moderation in Islamic zeal as the excesses of the Iranian Revolution became evident. Lecturers from overseas such as Rashid Ghannushi of Tunisia and Hassan Turabi of Sudan addressed large Muslim gatherings in the United States and began to identify the United States as *dar al-daʿwa* ("the abode of preaching"), *dar al-solh* ("the abode of treaty"), or *dar maftuha* ("an open country"), ready for the Islamic message. Both urged Muslims to participate in the United States, trusting in the message of Islam. Emphasizing the pluralistic nature of Islam and its amity with Christianity and Judaism, they urged the believers to be good citizens. There was no need for apprehension since there was no evidence of American persecution of Muslims. In fact, Ghannushi told Muslim audiences that they had more freedom in the United States to reflect on, discuss, and propagate their faith than was available in any Muslim nation.

A few small pockets of Muslims persist in believing that the United States is a *kafir* (infidel) nation. Those advocating such a perspective include the Tablighi Jamaʿat (Group of Informers), a group that started in India and spread throughout the world.[52] They renounce politics and focus on emulating the life of the Prophet. Another group is the supporters of the Salafi tradition of Saudi Arabia, who attempted with little success to recruit Muslims in the United States to their vision. A third group is Hizb al-Tahrir (Liberation Party), which started in Jordan and has spread to Europe with enthusiastic supporters among a fringe group of British Muslims and a few students on American campuses. All three groups insist that the Muslim community must maintain itself as an implant in a foreign body to ensure the separateness, difference, and distinction of Islam, as well as protection from the seductiveness of the American culture to the immigrants, converts, and their children.

Other groups, such as the Islamic Society of North America (ISNA), the Muslim American Society (MAS), and the Islamic Circle of North America (ICNA), who mostly adhere to the teachings of the Muslim Brotherhood of the Arab East and the Jama'ati Islami of the subcontinent, also started from the conviction that engagement with secular American society is to be avoided. ISNA moderated its stance in 1986 and began advocating participation in American society, albeit on Muslim terms. Both ISNA and ICNA have been engaged in various efforts of interfaith dialogue. ICNA and MAS have lately opened up their conventions to non- Muslim speakers.

The majority of Muslims in the United States (estimated at over 80 percent), however, are unmosqued; they have embraced the fact that they are part of American society and operate with little concern for what the compromise might cost. Many look with disdain at organized mosque centers and believe that non-practicing Muslims are on the right path just as much as those who attend regular mosque services. Thus, the challenges for the leadership of Muslim mosque organizations persist: Should they consider unmosqued Muslims as beyond the pale? Should Muslims strive for uniformity as they struggle to maintain unity and forge one community out of many? What options can be tolerated and still be considered within the scope of normative Islam? What shape should the ideal Muslim community take? Whose interpretation of these issues is authentic, and who has the authority to judge its validity?

While the new immigrants and the foreign "experts" were raising questions and debating the legitimacy of living in a non-Muslim state, the handful of imams who were in the United States were assuring their congregations that they have nothing to fear in the American context, since the United States is committed to democracy and religious freedom, hence promising Muslims a great future free from the supervision of autocratic regimes. Muhammad Abdul-Rauf, imam of the Islamic Center of Washington, D.C., warned against undue apprehension about the ability of Muslims to maintain the imperatives of Islamic life and practice in the United States. He considered efforts to create Islamic enclaves as unnecessary because of the promise of "the hospitable American melting pot" to make room for Muslims to create their own institutions and interpret their own faith in line with Islamic principles. He called on Muslims to look at the history of Islam and its tenacity and ability to withstand the cultural onslaught of fourteen centuries of alien cultures. America, he believed, makes room for Muslims, "not only to survive but also to flourish in honor and dignity."[53]

Others, spurred in part by the immigration of committed Muslims and by the intensifying anti-Muslim, anti-Arab atmosphere in the United States, reformulated their Arab-American identity and grounded it in Islam. One was Mohammad T. Mehdi (from Iraq), who first organized the Federation of Associations of Arab-American Relations to educate the American public and Congress about issues in the Middle East, and then the Action Committee on Arab-American Relations. An advocate of the American values of justice, freedom, and democracy, he became disillusioned with the effectiveness of Arab identity when the United States did not deliver on its promise of self-determination to the Palestinians.[54] He considered the creation of the state of Israel at the expense of the Palestinian people to be unjust. Mehdi later attempted to galvanize the diverse Muslim community to join him in reaching out to other Americans, expecting that the growing Muslim population from all over the world could provide additional popular support for his causes. Believing in the essential goodness of the American people, he was convinced that if they became aware of the injustices perpetrated against the Palestinians, financed and supported by the American taxpayers, American policy would change.[55] In his Islamic phase, he established the National Council of Islamic Affairs, an Islamic action committee that encouraged Muslims to run for office. (He set an example by running for a Senate seat in New York, where he received eighty-six thousand votes.) He accused the United

States of being silent about Israeli policies of "anti-gentilism" that discriminate against its Christian and Muslim population. He worked hard to incorporate Muslims into the American public square through networking, lobbying, and publishing pamphlets and books in support of his causes. He was extremely proud to see, after great effort, the crescent and star (as a symbol of Islam) displayed on the Ellipse in Washington next to the Christmas tree and the menorah.[56]

For Ismail al-Faruqi,[57] a Palestinian, the journey to Islamic identity unfolded in the American academy. With graduate degrees from Harvard and the University of Indiana, and post-doctoral studies at Al-Azhar University in Cairo, he began his career as a university professor. During the first phase of his intellectual journey, he believed in the power of Arabism as a culture and civilization to create a universal ethical system by promoting standards in human relations as enjoined in the Qur'an. For him, Arabism is not Arab nationalism or ethnocentrism, which developed under colonial rule, but an all-inclusive identity that is infused with Islamic values. It is not rooted in European ideologies of nationalism; rather, it is grounded in the Arabic Qur'an and shared by all Muslims whose culture, values, and ethos are inspired by its revelation.[58]

By the early 1970s, al-Faruqi began to share the general Arab disenchantment with Arab identity and turned to Islam. Reflecting on this period of his life, he reminisced, "There was a time in my life . . . when all I cared about was proving to myself that I could win my physical and intellectual existence from the West. But, when I won it, it became meaningless. I asked myself: Who am I? A Palestinian, a philosopher, a liberal humanist? My answer was: I am a Muslim."[59] From then on, he promoted Islam as the only umbrella ideology that can bring Muslims together. He criticized nationalism as an instrument used by the West to divide. Purified from its accretions and its compromises with Western colonialism, authentic Islam can bring about the revitalization of Muslim societies. In the process, Muslims need to avoid economic and political dependency, social and cultural emulation of the West, political fragmentation, and military impotence. The goal is to liberate Jerusalem and restore it to Muslim control.[60]

He became especially interested in the potential creation of a worldwide Muslim leadership in the United States. Besides mentoring large numbers of international graduate students at Temple University, he helped organize intellectual institutions dedicated to the task of "Islamizing knowledge." He argued that all knowledge is grounded in value systems. He believed that infusing the social sciences and the humanities with an Islamic foundation would help bring about the revival of Islam in the modern world. Toward this goal, he helped establish the American Association of Muslim Social Scientists, the International Institute of Islamic Thought in northern Virginia, and the Islamic College in Chicago to provide committed Islamic leadership, not only for the immigrant community, but more importantly, for the whole world of Islam. His writings were popular among a significant segment of Muslim students on American campuses, who found in them the way to maintain a distinctive identity that enhanced their strategy of survival in a hostile environment. Al-Faruqi recommended the appropriation of an Islamic ideology that emphasized that Muslims were not beggars in the United States, but active participants in the building of a just society. The adoption of an Islamic ideology was promoted as a mechanism to free the immigrant from the sense of guilt for achieving some measure of success in the United States.

At the same time, al-Faruqi sought to carve a space for Islam in the American religious mosaic by attempting to integrate Islam. He found the definition of America as a Judeo-Christian nation quite exclusionary, keeping Muslims outside the bounds of being fully recognized and celebrated citizens of the United States. He participated in interfaith dialogue with the World Council of Churches in Geneva[61] as well as various groups in the United States to promote the idea of dialogue among the "Abrahamic faiths." He emphasized that Judaism, Christianity, and Islam are grounded in the same source of faith, the God of Abraham.[62] He also sought to integrate Islam as a subject of study in the American

Academy of Religion by forming the Islamic Studies Section, which provided a venue for scholars to discuss Islam as a living faith in the United States and not as an alien "Oriental" religion.

Al-Faruqi also sought to construct a modern universal Islamic culture that is not only relevant, but also appealing in the American environment. He authored a book celebrating Muslim cultural achievement.[63] He disagreed with the sentiment among some immigrants that called for austerity and piety and the banning of music and art, and urged Muslims to surround themselves with Islamic decorations and artifacts in their homes and to participate in Islamic events such as *eid* celebrations. He believed that Muslims in the United States should adopt the practice prevalent among African-American Muslims and make the mosque a family-centered place where women attended and participated in mosque services. The mosque, he believed, should not only be the center for maintaining people in the faith, but also, and more importantly, should be crucial in fashioning the Muslim family, the most important social unit for the preservation of Islam in American society. Asked if he wanted to create a reformed Islam for North America, similar to Reformed Judaism, he replied, "No, my model is Conservative Judaism."[64]

By the middle of the 1980s, the Muslim immigrants who came in the post-1965 period stopped debating whether they could live in the United States and maintain their faith or should leave to live under the jurisdiction of an Islamic state. Rather, the discussion shifted to the definition of Muslim life in the American context—the institutions necessary for the maintenance of Muslim identity, and the scope of Muslim participation in the American public square. The debate among those in the community committed to practicing the faith in America centered on which model was to be emulated. The choice appeared to be between the Mennonite and the Jewish options. The Mennonites, despite their particular social, economic, cultural, and political outlook on life, were able to maintain their faith unchanged in the context of a secular state. The Jewish option was more appealing. The Jews represented a non-Christian religion whose approximately six million adherents had gained recognition as equal participants in fashioning the American society. Not only did American leaders talk about America as a Judeo-Christian country, but Jewish leadership was represented in the centers of power: in government, in the academy, and in all aspect of society. The Muslims wanted a similar place.

In 1993 a new organization came into existence, the North American Association of Muslim Professionals and Scholars (NAAMPS). At its inaugural meeting, Fathi Osman, an internationally recognized Islamic scholar who had for many years edited the London journal *Arabia*, spoke with confidence about the Muslim future in America. He envisioned a new role for Muslims, one grounded not in fear or isolation, but in engagement with society; not in retrenchment, but in exploration of new ways of leadership and participation. He saw the United States as an open venue for the development of new ideas and new visions. He challenged the Muslims of America blessed with this freedom to lead the revival of Islam in the world. He described the Muslims of the Arab world as ossified; they studied Islam of the past, while the Muslims of the United States had the capacity to be the pioneers of a new interpretation that would help solve the problems Muslims face. They could envision new and unlimited possibilities and help bring about a brighter future.[65]

Other speakers at the conference included Maher Hathout, president of the Islamic Center of Southern California, who called on Muslims to engage in realistic assessments of their problems and cease being fixated on the defense of Islam against its detractors. He reminded the community that the boundaries of isolation have not all been created by the suspicions of the larger society about Muslims, but that they were, in many cases, self-imposed out of fear. He urged the audience to reject separation and counseled reaching out to the larger community, to try and understand the American society. The first step in such an endeavor is to learn to listen, to alter the fixation with the rhetorical apologetic that Muslims have engaged in as a defense of Islam. He also counseled Muslims to engage in a more realistic and practical assessment of their condition rather than talk exclusively about ideals. Finally, he assured them that regardless of their efforts, their children were on the path of becoming American. "While we huddle together as Pakistanis or Egyptians or Iranians or whatever else, our children are, whether we believe it or like it or hate it or not, American kids. The question should be whether they will be Muslim-American kids or just American kids. Anyone who believes that he will raise an Egyptian boy in America is wrong: the maximum we can do is have a distorted Egyptian kid. The grandchildren will be without doubt American."[66]

A third speaker, Salam al-Marayati, also urged the audience to engage with America and take advantage of its freedom. He noted that his political activities on behalf of Muslims overseas were probably more effective than the combined effort of all the members of the Organization of the Islamic Conference. He urged Muslims to carve an "independent pathway." The choice is not between isolation and assimilation, but must be engagement with the society, taking America at its promise and working within the system to breach the walls of "the other."[67] "What good is our message, if we cannot deliver it to the world, to the humanity, or to the public? Contrarily, we cannot assimilate and lose our Islamic identity because we want to be involved in some ethnic group, or we think that is the American thing to do. . . . Yes, we must be Muslims, offer Islamic values, and be American citizens all in one."[68]

2

Muslims and American Religious Pluralism

◉

The September 11, 2001, attacks on the World Trade Center and the Pentagon have fostered new reflections on Islamic theological discourse throughout the Muslim world on issues of violence, tolerance, diversity, and pluralism. Some of the discourse was initiated as a response to the universal condemnation of the ideology the terrorists claimed as inspired by the teachings of Islam. The new discourse was initiated both overseas and in diaspora by Muslims disturbed by the yoking of Islam with militancy and terror. While Muslims overseas have generally continued to contextualize the violence as a reaction to American neocolonial policies in the Muslim world, for diaspora Muslims, given the current prevailing Islamophobia, the intricacies of the "why" of the violence have been sidelined in the effort to dissociate and distance themselves from the perpetrators. They have sought to repossess a role in defining their own faith and take it back from the extremists as well as those who thrive on demonizing Islam.

In response to a variety of events overseas that have tarred Muslims by association, a reexamination of the ideological constructs of diaspora Islam that have been in process since the beginning of Muslim emigration to the United States became urgent.

In the post-9/11 atmosphere, Muslims were confronted by rising xenophobia and Islamophobia, in part as a consequence of the propaganda for war. At the same time, such reflections became a necessity as government security measures targeted Arabs and Muslims through profiling, censoring of Islamic texts, monitoring of mosques, freezing of assets of Muslim NGOs, search and seizure, arrest, deportation, and rendition of suspects. Anxiety and marginalization engendered by these policies were also augmented by the demands of certain sectors of American society in the United States that the government has to get into religion building, to help reformulate the religion and promote a "moderate Islam," one that can fit the description of "the religion of peace."[1] Such measures left Muslims isolated, marginalized, and placed in what one Muslim called a "virtual internment camp."

Previous generations of immigrants, in contexts such as the Arab-Israeli conflict, the Salman Rushdie affair, and the Iranian Revolution, had to address similar charges against Islam and Muslims. The attacks of 9/11 have dealt a great setback to Muslim efforts to engage with American society by participating in the public square. The goal of these reflections is not only to prove that Muslims living in the West are loyal citizens, but more importantly that they share American values and are not associated with the teachings of those targeted in America's declared global war on terrorism, who have been variously labeled as extremist, fundamentalist, jihadist, terrorist, and proponents of an Islamo-fascist Islam.

The new diaspora discourse on pluralism displays a strong awareness of the need for a pluralistic interpretation of Qur'anic verses that have been utilized by extremists to justify their terrorist actions. This is crucial not only to assuage the doubts and apprehensions of the general public, but, more importantly, to address the reality of the diversity within the North American Muslim community itself and the challenge of forging a united front. Islam is projected by the community as a way of life, a culture, which as such provides guidance on issues of "diversity, unity, harmony, tolerance and peace."[2]

The response to the accusation that Islam is a violent religion has been addressed since the nineteenth century in various venues and in different languages throughout the Muslim world as Muslims have attempted to respond to the challenges of Western encroachment on their lands as well as their civilization and culture. The eagerness to showcase moderation, tolerance, and pluralism in Islam was not invented in the heat of the moment as a response to the intense scrutiny Islam and Muslims undergo during periods of crisis. Rather, it has a venerable place in the heritage of Islam. This literature asserts unequivocally that if some Muslims promote ideas of vengeance and hate in the name of Islam, it is due to their misunderstanding and misinterpretation of the Islamic sources, the teaching of the Qur'an and the Prophet Muhammad, as well as the historical record of Islamic civilization.

In the 1980s, the term *al-ta'addudiyya* was coined by Arab intellectuals to parallel the Western concept of pluralism. It was cast into the Arab market of ideas as a challenge to the growing Islamization of society and the demand for establishing an Islamic state and the adoption of the Shari'ah as the law of the state. Several conferences and symposia to consider the role of pluralism in Islamic thought, funded by European governments and civic organizations, were held in various Arab countries. As a consequence, *al-ta'addudiyya* became the buzzword of the nineties.[3] It joined a venerable list of concepts conceived and popularized in the West and idealized and exported for foreign consumption, such as modernity, democracy, nationalism, normalization, secularism, human rights, women's rights, minority rights, and privatization. These concepts are generally seen as challenges to developing countries, and their adoption a sign of having successfully joined the ranks of civilized nations.[4] Muslim intellectuals have been addressing these challenges as soon as they are posited, perceiving them as new hurdles to be cleared in an effort to prove that Islam not only measures up to Western norms, but is the pioneer in setting these norms. Authors generally rummage through Islamic history and texts searching for parallels they can recommend or sanctions that can be invoked to support their arguments. Their own differing ideological perspectives determine whether they see Western values as antithetical to, compatible with, or in fact the very essence of Islam.

This chapter will provide an overview of the wider context in which the discourse on pluralism in Islam concretized and the modern historical milieu that fostered reflections on the topic. It will provide a brief discussion of the Qur'anic verses used to buttress arguments to undergird the claims for Islamic pluralism. Contemporary Islamic interpretations that were incubated and nurtured overseas have been transplanted by Muslims living in diaspora. Whether consciously or unconsciously, these theological constructs of the meaning of certain Qur'anic verses and cultural norms formulated in particular contexts and responding to direct and indirect challenges are the intellectual sources and in some cases precedents of the discourse produced by writers in diaspora, especially by bicultural Muslim intellectuals, both immigrants and émigrés.

The last section of the chapter will focus on the material generated in diaspora among immigrant and convert Muslims who are responding to the impugning by the Western public of Islam and its teachings post-9/11. The need to focus on and emphasize the diversity of Muslims becomes an imperative as Western governments appear to hold their Muslim citizens potentially guilty by association with a faith that has been deemed by some as beyond the pale. There appears to be an incipient hope, if not expectation, that once Western societies are enlightened about the true nature of Islamic pluralism, they will incorporate Islam and Muslim culture, not as a novelty consigned to ghettoes of difference, but as an integral part of Western society.

Pluralism and the Muslim Encounter with Colonialism

The Muslim encounter with colonialism is part of the identity formation of most Muslims in today's world. It is an essential part of the modern efforts at nation building in Muslim countries, having a prominent place in history and civics textbooks. The encounter is portrayed as violent in nature, with powerful Western armies encroaching on and subduing peaceful Muslims in an effort to monopolize their natural resources, restructure their economies, and gain strategic advantage over other competing European nations. The colonial venture and Muslim resistance to subjugation have given rise to a literature that analyzes the motives of European colonialism as masked under the guise of the benevolent project of bringing democracy to people living under autocratic rule, liberating the women of Islam from bondage to men, providing modern education, and fostering civic organizations in order to uplift Muslim societies. Whether operating under the banner of the French "civilizing mission" or the British "white man's burden," Western expansion into Muslim territories is at times depicted as having a religious agenda carried out by colonial bureaucrats and Christian missionaries, considered the two "archenemies of Islam" who sought to liberate Muslims from Islam.[5] Thus, colonialism is held culpable for defaming Islam and projecting its own aggression onto Muslims, promoting ethnic and sectarian divisions as part of the policy of divide and rule. The colonial venture is seen as anything but pluralistic. It promoted division and sectarianism while insisting that the Western worldview was superior and must supersede all others. Colonial bureaucrats aimed at restructuring Islamic societies and casting them in their own image. The authors insist that the pluralism Western nations do not practice what they preach. A current manifestation is the mistreatment of Islam and Muslims who live in the West, who continue to be held responsible for the acts of extremists overseas. Just as nationalism was invented by the West to divide the Muslim world into discreet entities, pluralism is seen as a recasting of the perennial efforts by the West to undermine Islam.

A significant amount of Islamic literature produced throughout the twentieth century is defensive and polemic in tone. It addresses the issues raised about the adequacy, efficacy, and validity of Islam as a religion for the modern world, one that can generate a renaissance to confront the new challenges facing Islamic societies and bring them to parity with the West. It responds to Western charges that Islam advocates holy war, *jihad*, against non-Muslims and has legislated subjugation of women and minorities. As a response, the modernist reformer Muhammad 'Abduh insisted that Islam favors forgiveness and that fighting is sanctioned only for putting an end to aggression against Islam and Muslims, as well as to maintain peace. Jihad, he argued, is not aimed at forcing people to convert to Islam, or to punish those who disagree with Muslims. He distinguished between the Christian and the Muslim history of conquest. Christian history, he wrote, is noted for its massacres, the killing of old men, women, and children. Muslims, however, can boast that there has not been a single Islamic war that sought the annihilation of others. When Muslims conquered a territory, they practiced Islamic tolerance and allowed its people to worship and practice their faith and maintain their customs. While it is true that non-Muslims were required to pay the *jizya*, or poll tax, they were guaranteed security and protection in return.[6] Muslim rulers instructed Muslim armies to respect those who were in convents and monasteries, and proclaimed the sanctity of the blood of women, children, and noncombatants. The teaching of the Prophet forbids hurting non-Muslims, *dhimmis*; the Prophet Muhammad said that "he who harms a *dhimmi* is not one of us."[7]

Pluralism and the Encounter with the Cold War

By the middle of the twentieth century, the colonial and the missionary presence in Muslim nations came to an end. Islamic literature increasingly referred to the colonial incursion as part of the "intellectual or cultural invasion," *al-ghazu al-thaqafi*.[8] It portrayed Western educational, cultural, and social institutions introduced in Muslim nations as part of a sustained campaign to root out religion. Western leaders were accused of not being satisfied with military and political domination, but aiming at the eradication of Islam—its culture, civilization, and intellectual expression. Thus, Westerners did not practice pluralism or promote equality between Western and Islamic cultures. Rather, they assumed the roles of teachers, reformers, and enforcers of their own ideas and beliefs, and claimed that Western values are universal and all alternative values must aspire to match their level.

The Marxist challenge of the middle of the twentieth century was seen by the Islamists as promoting radical secularization and the eradication of any vestiges of religion. Those promoting Westernization and advocates of nationalism and socialism were accused of having bought into this kind of antireligious ideology and thereby been duped by outside forces bent on destroying Islam.[9]

The most important advocate of Islamic supersession, whose works have been translated and disseminated throughout the world, was Sayyid Qutb. He originally advocated Islam as an alternative to capitalism and Marxism, but later revised his ideology and decreed an Islamic imperative, a comprehensive, holistic vision that offered Islamic answers to social, economic, political, and cultural problems. He promoted the idea of an Islamic imperative, one that supersedes both materialistic systems, capitalism and Marxism. Islamism asserts a parallel claim of a promise of a better future, one promised by God to the believers, a promise that has been vindicated in history, as demonstrated by the greatness of the Islamic empires. Qutb attacked what he saw as the perversion of Christianity. In *Fi Zilal al-Qur'an* he depicted Christians as extremists because of their claim that God has a son.[10] He accused them of being duplicitous for their refusal to govern by the laws and dictates that God has revealed, preferring to follow their own whims. For Qutb, governing by any law other than the Shari'ah amounts to disobedience and apostasy.[11] As the final revelation from God, the Qur'an abrogates and supersedes all other revelations.[12] Thus, he viewed the world from a bipolar perspective: the abode of Islam, *dar al-Islam*, where Islamic law is implemented regardless of the religious affiliation of the citizens, and the abode of war, *dar al-harb*, where Islamic law is not implemented.[13] This sets up the justification of using violence against those who do not govern by what God has revealed.

Thus, while Abduh had defended Islam against the accusations of intolerance and aggression and promoted the idea of

Islam as peace, Qutb, writing in the context of torture in Nasser's prisons in the 1960s, justified jihad as armed resistance. For decreeing laws based on socialist ideology, Nasser was deemed an apostate, and thus it was just to struggle against his system, which violated God's dictates. Qutb argued that the sword verses (S. 9:5, 29, 36) constituted the final revelation dealing with the relation of Muslims to non-Muslims. People of the Book (Jews and Christians), having sanctioned what has been forbidden by God, are called unbelievers, *kuffar*. They have forfeited their right to protection; they must either convert to Islam or pay the *jizya*. Those who refuse can be killed, and Muslims who emulate the deviant ways of the People of the Book can expect the same fate.[14] Qutb wrote that the Qur'an warns Muslims about the reality of their enemies and of the war they wage against Muslims because of their doctrine.[15] While Muslims are asked to be tolerant of the People of the Book, they are not to take them as friends.[16] Qutb was dubious about efforts at dialogue and compromise. Those who seek to bring about good relations among religious people misunderstand the meaning of religion. Islam alone is acceptable, and no other religion can be recognized.[17] Therefore, no covenant with people of other faiths can be accepted unless it has this condition.[18] Furthermore, the Islamic imperative does not tolerate coexistence with falsehood. It must obliterate all impediments while providing freedom of choice. True liberation comes when people choose Islam out of conviction.[19]

The 1967 Arab defeat in the Six-Day War brought about a major reassessment and self-critical literature in the Arab world that blamed Arab failure on the premise that the nation-states had put their faith in nationalism and socialism and abandoned Islam. Some authors wrote that the Israelis were victorious because of their devotion to their religion and their insistence on fashioning a Jewish state, while Muslims had abandoned the idea of a Muslim state. This soon gave way to anticolonial, anti-imperialist, and anti-Zionist themes centering on mobilization of the masses who were disenchanted with the new international order with the United Nations as an arbiter of justice, since it allowed Israel to hold on to lands conquered through a "pre-emptive strike." This was perceived as a conspiracy against Muslim rights and a violation of United Nations universal proclamations. It was time to reassess, to grieve over a loss of innocence, to mourn fresh victims and the death of hope. The international order does not treat Muslims and non-Muslims equally.[20]

With the death of Nasser, Sadat became president. He removed the socialists from positions of power, brought the Islamists out of prison, and gave them a prominent role in society. For him, Islamism was the firewall necessary to hold socialism at bay. Once set free, Islamists demanded the establishment of an Islamic state in Egypt and the implementation of the Shari'ah as the law of the land. The Shari'ah, they believed, would place restrictions on the legislative authority of the ruler. It was seen as the only way to curb the excesses of Nasser, Sadat, and later Mubarak. For them, the Qur'anic verse "This day, I have perfected your religion for you and completed my favor upon you and chosen Islam as your religion" (S. 5:3) provided a divine sanction for the primacy and supersession of Islam over all other religions, ideologies, and systems. Even the venerable al-Azhar, the intellectual center of Sunni Islam, generally accountable to the authorities in power, issued a statement on the subject: "Not to implement the revelation in God's Book and judge by His decrees is *kufr* (unbelief). If a person refuses to believe in it, doubts its divine origin, professes that it is not valid for judgment, ridicules it, says that it is inappropriate except for the society or the age in which it was revealed, or [is guilty of] other similar statements or actions, he transgresses the ordinances of God."[21]

This interpretation persists in the ideologies of Islamic revolutionary groups such al-Takfir wa al-Hijra, al-Jihad Islami, al-Qaeda, and the Taliban. These groups continue to condemn those who do not subscribe to their interpretation of Islam as *kuffar*, persons who willfully and intentionally conceal the truth of Islam.

The militancy and violence of these groups evoked a response within Islamist circles.[22] A new vision began to be formulated, one that attempted not necessarily to replicate what obtained in medieval Islamic states, but to create a modern ideological state that could resist the encroachment of Marxism, one that would not tolerate alternative ideologies. From this perspective Islam was posited as an ideological system, not a set of doctrines, beliefs, and practices. Muslims were subject to a divine mandate to implement this system in the world and to eradicate all other systems, which by definition must be considered ungodly. These ideas cohered during the Cold War as Marxism and capitalism squared off, each claiming exclusive possession of universal truth, each declaring eternal enmity to the other while striving to impose its vision on the rest of the world. The emphasis shifted from Islam as the middle religion, a formulation promoted by the reformers of the early twentieth century, to Islam as divinely chartered and sanctioned to resist the onslaught of both systems that claimed sole possession of the truth in an attempt to impose their values and their norms on other nations. Each demanded total adherence to its vision, each was unrelenting in its claim to monopoly on the truth, each rejected pluralism as an option.

Pluralism Debates in the Aftermath of the Iranian Revolution

The 1979 Islamic Revolution in Iran jolted Western nations as they began to reassess the reality of Islamic militancy and the power of Islamic ideology to garner the devotion of the masses and undermine puppet regimes. The success of the revolution fueled Islamist groups throughout the Muslim world who preached that God will give the victory to those who believe, if they but believe. The ability of the Iranian Revolution to get rid of the shah, depicted as the mightiest of tyrants, protected by the United States, the most powerful nation, could be replicated if Muslims focused on being better Muslims and resisted efforts to impose foreign values. The success of the revolution provided a formula for victory, a prototype that could be replicated in other places under puppets accountable to American interests. Islamic groups began to demand the institution of an Islamic state, and concomitant hostility was generated toward Christians, who were not happy with such developments. Books were published critiquing Christian doctrine, and Christian properties came under attack.

One of the most influential of the contemporary Islamists is Muslim Brotherhood activist Yusuf al-Qaradawi. His 1983 *Ghayr al-Muslimin fi al-Mujtama' al-Islami* was published during a tense period in Egypt when Islamic groups were harassing the minority Coptic Christian community.[23] Al-Qaradawi based his analysis on the historical precedent of the covenant, *'ahd*, through which People of the Book are guaranteed security by the Muslim state even though they are not forced to convert. Thus, Copts can still enjoy Islamic citizenship and the freedom to practice their own faith at the same time that they are subject to Islamic law. They are guaranteed personal and communal security, and their property rights must be respected. He based this on S. 60:8-9, which affirms the essential Islamic principles of toleration, justice, and mercy.[24] Muslims therefore do not have the right to punish those who hold to differing doctrines.[25] People of the Book, while enjoying these rights in an Islamic state, have specific duties under the Shari'ah. Among them is the paying of the poll tax, *jizya*. Some had argued that this tax was imposed by God because of the basic inferiority of the People of the Book due to their refusal to accept the religion of Islam, but al-Qaradawi interprets it rather as a way in which Christians can contribute to the welfare of the state, since they are not drafted into the army and are not subject to the obligations of *zakat* and *jihad*. Furthermore, non-Muslims must be subject to the regulations of the Shari'ah; specifically they cannot collect interest on their investments; cannot be involved in any occupations that involve the selling or importing of forbidden substances, such as alcohol or pork; and cannot hold official positions of a religious nature, such as head of state, or judge among Muslims. Also, Christians must not offend the religious sensibilities of Muslims by wearing or showing their religious symbols in obvious or inappropriate ways. This includes the proscription on displaying crosses or other Christian paraphernalia in public places, or demonstrating their religion too overtly. Christians must not consume wine or pork publicly or sell such commodities to Muslims, and they must not speak negatively about Islam.[26] This principle of not offending religious sensibilities, however, is not reciprocal. Muslims do not have to be sensitive to Christians if this requires ignoring the commandments of God in the effort not to offend the People of the Book. Tolerance does not mean that the essential differences between religions should be ignored. The essential oneness of God must be affirmed at all times, the Christian notion of the Trinity notwithstanding. Stressing of commonalities can lead to contradiction, separation, and even destruction.[27]

Such reflections became necessary in opposition to Islamist rhetoric used by thinkers such as Egyptian Sayyid Qutb,[28] ideologue of the Muslim Brotherhood in the 1960s, and Abu al-A'la al-Mawdudi,[29] founder of the Jama'ati Islami Movement in Pakistan, and Islamist groups such as Jihad Islami, Takfir wa Hijra, and Qutbiyyun, which had set the tone for an Islamist ideological discourse that continues to be advocated by Islamic revolutionary groups.[30]

By the middle of the 1980s, Western funding became available for conferences and symposia addressing the topic of pluralism in the Arab world. The term *ta'addud* was first used by secular Arab nationalists. (Earlier usage was mainly in reference to multiple wives, *ta'addud al-zawjat*.) *Ta'addud* was first used as part of the title of a symposium convened by the Jordanian Center for Research and Information in 1986.[31] Several other symposia followed in Jordan and Egypt.[32] By the 1990s, discourse on pluralism had become indigenized. Islamists were using the term to explore issues of conflict and difference in Islamic society as well as the legitimacy of a multiparty system in an Islamic state.[33] In 1992, the Labor Party in Egypt held a symposium on Islam and Pluralism.[34] By 1993, Dr. Muhyi al-Din 'Atiyyah, editor of *al-Muslim al-Mu'asir* magazine, compiled a bibliography of 122 titles related to pluralism.[35]

In their debates, Islamists have addressed such matters as universal pluralism, whether the Islamic state can maintain normal relations with governments who promote non-Islamic or un-Islamic ideas and practices; political pluralism, whether the

Islamic polity can tolerate political differences within its ranks without disobeying the commandments of God; sectarian pluralism, whether the Islamic majority, the Sunnis, can tolerate the differences in religious interpretation represented by Islamic sectarian groups; gender pluralism, whether women have a public role in an Islamic state and when they can be allocated equal rights to those of men; and religious pluralism, whether the Muslim nation can afford equal status and opportunities for religious minorities (Christians) in a reconstituted Islamic state, allowing them the role they acquired under nationalist governments.[36] The pluralism discourse also addressed such issues as peaceful rotation of authority, public approval through elections and nominations, separation among the several branches of government, peaceful coexistence among various groups, and respect for human rights.[37] Islamists have also developed new and moderate positions, such as a pluralistic vision that allows for the rotation of leadership among different parties and a call for new jurisprudence that incorporates the People of the Book as full citizens in a Muslim state.

In Egypt, the discourse focused on the role of minorities in a Muslim majority state. Muhammad al-'Awwa rejected the depiction of Egypt as having two peoples, Muslims and Copts, as untrue and fraught with the danger of stoking the fires of division. He quoted a legal scholar of the early twentieth century who wrote, "When we speak of the Islamic *ummah*, I do not mean to refer exclusively to the society of Muslims only, rather, I refer to a distinctive society which is a historical product of the cooperative efforts of all the religious sects which have lived and worked together under the banner of Islam and which has presented us with a corporate heritage for all the inhabitants of the Islamic East."[38]

Joining the debate, the journalist Fahmi Huwaydi noted that the Qur'anic text is very clear about human relations and must be distinguished from the accretion of interpretations. The Qur'an unequivocally states that God created Adam and hence humans to be his vicegerents on earth. It does not specify that this is a role for Muslims alone. Vicegerency on earth is assigned to all human beings, as all are creatures of God. This guarantees that minorities have full rights in a truly Islamic state.[39] He strongly disagreed with those who said that respecting the legitimacy or the rights of others means that one has to give credence to their beliefs. He cited a number of Qur'an verses to prove the mandate to recognize the existence of other persons and communities,[40] and on the basis of those verses he worked out an Islamic definition of brotherhood. All men are creatures and vicegerents of God, as the Qur'an affirms, and thus minorities should be accorded full rights in an Islamic state.[41]

While God could have created one uniform universal system, he decreed a perpetual pluralism in civilizations, systems, and laws (S. 5:48, 69). It is his divine will that different cultures compete in striving to bring about a virtuous society. From this perspective, Islam does not seek the negation or the eradication of "the other," since God created difference as a means of fostering competition in virtue among the nations, a fact that guarantees progress (S. 2:251).[42] Furthermore, God favors moderation, as is demonstrated in the fact that he made the Muslim community (*ummatan wasat*) a middle community, one that avoids extremes. And, unlike Christianity, Islam provides for freedom of religious thought. Even though a statement by a Muslim appears in a hundred ways to make him a *kafir*, or unbeliever, if there is even one way that can be accepted as belief, then he cannot be called an unbeliever.[43]

The discourse defined pluralism as the affirmation of difference, of freedom, and of peaceful coexistence. "Pluralism in its general philosophy is a natural truth, a universal law, a legal way of life and a divine mercy."[44] It was promoted as a foundational principle of nature, as evident in the revelation of the Qur'an, which affirmed the equality of all humanity, regardless of color, language, rights, or lineage; all are equal before the law. Thus, the advocacy of pluralism became the essence of the divine plan for humanity as revealed in the Qur'an. The Qur'an revealed that one of God's signs is his creation of the world as composed of different nations, ethnicities, tribes, and languages (S. 30:22; 48:13). Difference in the divine plan is not for discord or war, but a sign of God's mercy that humans may have a better understanding of one another; or, as Fahmi Huwaydi puts it, Islam is pluralistic "because he [God] willed us to be different."[45]

Muslim Diaspora Discourse on Pluralism

The Muslim authors who have addressed issues of pluralism in the United States have done so mostly in the confines of academia. The majority are immigrants or émigrés from all over the Muslim world who have found a home in the United States and a conducive environment to research, reflect, and publish without the constraints of government censorship. The earliest to address the issue of pluralism in Islam were Fazlur Rahman and Isma'il al-Faruqi, both émigrés who were unable to return to their home countries due to political exigencies: Rahman because he was deemed too liberal by a Pakistani government bent on cobbling together an Islamic state after the war of independence, and al-Faruqi, because he had been a governor of Galilee, which was seized by the Israelis. Both had an international reputation and became very influential as Muslim students from all over the Muslim world flocked to study under their guidance on American campuses. To varying degrees, they participated in interfaith dialogue and, at times, trialogue, where they became engaged in defending the faith against its American detractors and responding to their colleagues' challenges.

Al-Faruqi was initially an advocate of Arab nationalism, but, disappointed by America's response to the 1967 Israeli pre-emptive attack on three Arab states, which he saw as aggression against the rights of the Palestinian people, he lost hope that Palestinian rights would be redressed through U.N. and U.S. mediation. He came to embrace an Islamist ideology in the early 1970s.

For al-Faruqi, Islamic civilization is a witness to Muslim tolerance and provides an actual model of a culture where other religions have thrived. "The *modus vivendi* which Islam provided for the world religions in Madinah, Damascus, Cordoba, Cairo, Delhi and Istanbul is certainly worthy of emulation by the whole world."[46] Islam respects Judaism and Christianity, their founders and scriptures, not out of courtesy or the necessity of social, political, cultural or civilizational concerns, but as a foundational acknowledgment of religious truth. They are not "other views" that need to be tolerated, but *de jure*, "truly revealed religions from God. . . . In this Islam is unique. For no religion in the world has yet made belief in the truth of other religions a necessary condition of its own faith and witness."[47]

Al-Faruqi asserted that Islam's contribution to interreligious dialogue in the world is "very, very significant." Islam has experience in the field with the widest variety of religions and ethnicities. Starting with its relationship with Judaism and Christianity, as prescribed in the Qur'an, it extended its engagement and tolerance to other religions based on the shared beliefs in God and the Qur'anic affirmation that all human beings are religious by nature.[48] This he based on the idea of Islam as *din al-fitra*, that religion is innate to human nature. "For the first time it has become possible for the adherent of one religion to tell an adherent of another religion: 'We are both equal members of a universal religious brotherhood. Both of our traditional religions are *de jure*, for they are both issued from and are based upon a common source, the religion of God which He has implanted equally in both of us, upon *din al-fitrah*.'"[49] From this perspective, the Muslim does not look at the non-Muslim as "a fallen, hopeless creature, but a perfect man capable by himself of achieving the highest righteousness."[50]

Al-Faruqi did not think that Christians reciprocated these sentiments. He dismissed Vatican II as "too modest a contribution," as it did not engage seriously in dialogue. While it may have stopped calling non-Christians by bad names, this was not necessarily a great achievement, since politeness in modern society is a prerequisite, as are courtesy and mutual respect. The assertion of deference for Islam is not sufficient to produce an "admiring trance"; it still places the Muslims with the archaic religions.[51] After fourteen centuries, Vatican II in a "condescending and paternalizing manner" decreed "that Islam is a tolerable approximation of Christianity" while asserting that salvation can be found

only within the church.[52] While al-Faruqi promoted ideas of tolerance and a pluralistic interpretation of the Qur'anic verses, he felt
that it was the duty of Muslims in the United States to propagate
the faith and share their beliefs with Americans because they had
a message that could elevate American society. "For the Muslim,
the relation of Islam to the other religions has been established by
God in his revelation, the Qur'an. No Muslim therefore may deny
it; since for him the Qur'an is the ultimate authority."[53]

As Muslims were once again called upon to address issues of
pluralism, diversity, and tolerance in the 1980s and were pressured about the treatment of religious minorities in Iran's Islamic
Republic, al-Faruqi cautioned that religion and politics should
be separate. "Do not mix up Islam with Iran. Do not say in one
breath Islam and events in Saudi Arabia." He gave the example of
the internment of the Japanese during World War II as a political expedient similar to the treatment of minorities in Iran and
Saudi Arabia.[54]

Fazlur Rahman of the University of Chicago based his
responses on a reinterpretation of the Qur'anic verses that advocated supersession. He noted that the Qur'an deplores the fact
that religions are divided within themselves, as well as from each
other. Humankind was one, but the split came with the advent
of prophets with their messages. While these messages became the
divisive force, the difference was part of the divine mystery (S.
2:213). The Qur'an leaves no room for exclusivist claims by various faith communities (S. 2:211, 113, 120). "The Qur'an's reply
to those exclusivist claims of proprietorship over God's guidance,
then, is absolutely unequivocal: Guidance is not the function of
communities but of God and good people, and no community
may lay claims to be uniquely guided and elected" (S. 2:124).[55]

The central verse that advocates pluralism is S. 5:48, which
demonstrates universal goodness with the belief in one God and
the day of judgment, and mandates that "the Muslim community
be recognized as a community among communities."[56] Although
the Qur'an states that the Muslim community is "the best community produced for mankind" (S. 3:110), this status does not

guarantee that Muslims "will be automatically God's darling," for unless they maintain welfare for the poor and work for righteousness, God will substitute a different people in their place.[57]

Pluralism Discourse in the 1990s

The fall of the Soviet Union and the Rushdie affair in 1989 brought about dramatic changes in the comfort zone of Muslims, who began to feel targeted by the Western media as intolerant and unfit for citizenship in the United States. The splintering of the Soviet Empire propelled the United States into the role of the only superpower in the world, leaving Muslim nations who had mastered the game of survival by playing the United States against the Soviet Union wondering about their future. It also fostered speculation about the identity of the next enemy that would need to be vanquished by the United States. The publication of Samuel P. Huntington's article "The Clash of Civilizations?,"[58] which proposed that the West would be confronted by Islamic civilization, raised Muslims' level of concern throughout the world. This was exacerbated by the publication of *The Satanic Verses* by Salman Rushdie, in which Muslims perceived him to be defaming the Prophet Muhammad. This elicited a *fatwa* by Ayatollah Khomeini, who declared Rushdie an apostate whose killing would be sanctioned by Islamic law. The Western reaction to the *fatwa* was swift and unequivocal. Many Muslims in diaspora felt targeted by the press, their religion deemed deficient and archaic since it prescribed death to those who deviated from the accepted orthodoxy.

This propelled more Muslim authors to become engaged in writing about pluralism, including such authors as Fathi Osman and Abdulaziz Sachedina, who advocated a pluralistic Islam, grounded not in fear or isolation but in engagement with American society and exploration of new ways of leadership and participation in it.

For Osman, the theology of pluralism begins with the affirmation that all humans are descended from the same pair. The Qur'an talks about the dignity of all humans as "children of Adam," even though they may not believe in God. He concedes that consensus on all matters is impossible and that different views will continue to prevail because God willed it that way. Meanwhile, he holds that "God's grace lies not in the abolition of difference in beliefs and views, nor in changing human nature which He himself has created, but in showing human beings how to handle their differences intellectually and morally and behaviorally."[59] In defending Islam against its detractors as well as the extremists, Osman reinforced his theology of pluralism and the freedom of difference by pointing out that there is no reference in the Qur'an to meting out death for apostasy; rather, death is imposed for crimes against the state. "Freedom of belief cannot be genuinely secured," he says, "unless abandoning the faith is unrestricted, the same as embracing it is not imposed."[60]

Abdulaziz Sachedina of the University of Virginia published his seminal work *The Islamic Roots of Democratic Pluralism* prior to the attacks of 9/11. He noted that the Qur'an provides a basis for a democratic pluralistic global community. The universal Islamic model demands coexistence among people of different religions as part of the divine plan for humanity.[61] He noted that Islam has a unique characteristic that proceeds from the unity of God, a fact that unites the Muslim community with all humanity.[62] Pluralism is thus part of the divine mystery, and as such it means not merely tolerating difference, but accepting others "in fellowship towards the divine."[63] He, too, saw this foundational principle of the Qur'an as having been obscured by the doctrine of supersession devised by the traditional exegetes. They claimed that the verses of the Qur'an that promote pluralism were abrogated by others revealed at a later date. However, "of the 137 listed verses that are claimed to have been abrogated, in reality not even one of them has been abrogated."[64] Furthermore, he noted that the Qur'an assures Christians and Jews who believe in God and the Last Day that they will be saved (S. 2:62); there is nothing in the Qur'an that suggests that it abrogated the previous scriptures of the Jews and the Christians.[65]

Building on the same Qur'anic reference used by al-Faruqi of the Islamic concept of *din al-fitra*, Sachedina argued that the fact that *fitra* affirms that each human being is endowed with a sense of knowledge and discernment of good and evil, as well the relationship of humans to the divine, suggest that all humanity has a bond in being predisposed toward monotheism. He faulted the two major branches of Islam, Sunni and Shi'a, for impeding human progress, the Sunnis by affirming and practicing exclusivism and the Shi'a by insisting on certain prerequisites and qualifications for the interpreters of the Qur'an. Their exclusive claims to truth have impeded human recognition of the divine mandate for pluralism, which can promote peace in a violent world.[66]

Writing prior to 9/11, Abou El Fadl, in *The Authoritative and the Authoritarian*, also addressed the issue of tolerance within the Muslim community in the United States. He wrote that the Qur'an makes it quite clear that the truth is accessible to all people regardless of gender, class, or race. He was criticized not only for airing dirty laundry in public, but for being critical of certain Islamic interpretations at a time when Muslims were under undue pressure from Western writers such as Huntington and Islamophobes such as Daniel Pipes, as well as from those who adhered to an exclusivist Wahhabi Islam.[67]

Beginning in the 1990s, a new crop of university professors became employed at American universities. Three that have written on pluralism come from Africa—from Gambia, the Sudan, and South Africa. Each has made a distinctive contribution to the debates that bears the imprint of their African experience.

Surveying the writings of public intellectuals of the last decade of the twentieth century, Sulayman S. Nyang of Howard University sees an accelerated interest in pluralism as a consequence of changes taking place in the world. He identifies three converging realities that push toward pluralism: globalization, which has brought humanity closer together by tearing down the walls of separation, a phenomenon caused by the communication revolution; growing awareness by the poor of the world of the material possibilities that they then began to seek; dissatisfaction with secularism and a growing quest for spiritual meaning; and an increased awareness of other religions now gathered under the same roof as a consequence of international migration.

At the same time, he identifies five factors that have limited the Muslim response to pluralism and impeded their relishing of American values. In the first place, Muslims, like American conservatives, are repulsed by American popular culture, which they see as a "libertinism" that allows sexual promiscuity. They are also turned off by American materialism, which places a premium on "excessive acquisitiveness." Furthermore, they find American textbooks problematic; they "wish to keep their children from the triple problems of religious indoctrination, drugs, and sexual promiscuity" and seek to remove anti-Muslim materials from the textbooks. They are also reluctant to embrace "excessive individualism," which they perceive as undermining the importance of the family and the maintenance of a cohesive society. They seek to maintain dietary restrictions, in part as a protection against gluttony. "In the special case of American Muslims, those who adhere faithfully to the halal diet see fewer opportunities in the eateries than their more voracious neighbors, who consume swine as easily as they imbibe alcohol."[68]

Despite such impediments to enthusiastic engagement in American pluralism, Nyang enjoins Muslim leaders to participate in dialogue over issues of common concern with the larger population. He especially puts the onus on them to share their particular perspective on life and urges them to participate in forums on American campuses and reach out to their neighbors and co-workers.[69] Nyang notes that "triumphant Islam" has tended to forget that Islam at its core, in its Meccan formative period, was pluralistic, and a true return to the teachings of the Qur'an and the practice of the prophet Muhammad would not lead to compelling others to follow one doctrine; rather, it would promote freedom of religion as proclaimed in the Qur'an: "There is no compulsion in religion."[70]

Another African intellectual who has found a home in the American academy is Farid Esack. While seeking inclusion of race in a pluralistic definition of Islam, Farid Esack writes out of the context of the struggle for liberation in South Africa. For him, pluralism includes an economic ingredient, the liberation from economic exploitation of people "who eke out an existence on the margins of society."[71] He prescribes pluralism as action to liberate people, not mere "joyous intellectual neutrality," but an endeavor to liberate and work toward healing societies that are racially divided, patriarchal, and economically exploitative. Esack faults traditional exegesis for promoting the doctrine of superses- sion, which has circumvented the Qur'anic verses that promote the recognition of other religions. Pluralism for Esack does not mean the liberal embrace of all "others" as equal. "The struggle in South Africa has demonstrated that some interpretations must be opposed because they suppress people."[72]

Another Muslim author from Africa is Abdullahi An-Na'im, professor of Islamic Studies at Emory University and a disciple of Mahmoud Taha, founder of the Republican Brothers, who was executed by the Sudanese government because his liberal ideas were deemed heretical.[73] In the United States, An-Na'im has insisted that Muslims need to generate new ideas in order to mainstream Islam and make it consistent with currently accepted universal norms. Rather than insisting that the world should adjust to their norms, which were formulated in a different con- text centuries ago, or reformulating and enwrapping them with modern discourse that maintains their superiority, Muslims need to align Islamic values with universal norms. He insists that the status of non-Muslim religious minorities under the Shari'ah is not congruent with current universal standards of human rights and cannot be justified by claims of Islamic cultural relativism. Religious minorities should not be subject to Muslim cultural norms that are not consistent with the relevant universal standards, and it is not only possible, but also imperative, that the status of non-Muslims under the Shari'ah be reformed from within the fundamental sources of Islam, namely the Qur'an and Sunnah. Such reform would at once be both Islamic and fully consistent with universal human rights standards.[74] He is therefore critical of Muslim insistence on implementing the Shari'ah, which he finds as discriminatory against non-Muslims since it renders them inferior and teaches that their lesser status is divinely mandated. "It would be heretical," he writes, "for a Muslim who believes the *shari'ah* is the final and ultimate formulation of the law of God to maintain that any aspect of that law is open to revision and reformulation by mere mortal and fallible human beings. To do so is to allow human beings to correct what God has decreed."[75]

At issue for An-Na'im are several laws and practices that the Shari'ah uses to restrict religious minorities. He notes that religious minorities "are not allowed to participate in the public affairs of an Islamic state. They are not allowed to hold any position of authority over Muslims, although Muslims may, and do, hold such positions over *dhimmis*. *Dhimmis* may practice their religion in private, but they are not allowed to proselytize or preach their faith in public. A *dhimmi* is allowed and even encouraged to embrace Islam while a Muslim may never abandon Islam."[76] The modern world has necessitated a revision of the Shari'ah, since the problems have changed and the traditional answers are no longer valid.[77]

The Pluralism Discourse after 2001

In the post-9/11 world, many Muslims increasingly see Western governments as hypocritical in their promotion of pluralism. They perceive governments as positing universal values and advocating adherence to them, while at the same time undermining them if they conflict with their national interest. Muqtedar Khan of the University of Delaware, for example, has noted that the United States uses pluralism as an ideology that it seeks to impose on less powerful nations as part of its global reach. In a sense, it is a tool of propaganda that supersedes truth and belies its power relationship with the Muslim world. The United States does not seek real international pluralism; it does not tolerate other views.[78]

Muslim reflections on American hypocrisy centrally take into consideration the so-called universal values (pluralism, democracy, human rights, the rights of minorities and women) advocated by the U.S. State Department as the foundation for relations with peoples of the Middle East.[79] An interested observer does not have to look far to find egregious violations of these stated values. America's promotion of democracy was undermined, for instance, by its rejection of the will of the Algerian and Palestinian people when they voted for Islamist representatives.

Muslims also wonder why the Western governments are silent when the demonization of Islam is given sensational play in the Western press. Post-9/11, the media played an important role in shaping negative American perceptions of Islam by featuring a slew of Muslims who were disenchanted with their religious tradition and were willing to voice the criticisms that the Islamophobes had been spreading about the evil intents of Islam and Muslims living in the West. They were championed as "native informers" who validated all the fears and stereotypes perpetrated about the faith.

Writing from the U.K., Mona Siddiqui has also reflected on this topic. She notes that 9/11 managed to convince onlookers that religious expression can be associated with religious fanaticism and that Muslim fanaticism is anti-American and therefore a global threat.[80] In effect, Siddiqui says, Western discussions on pluralism are the product of Western developments after the Enlightenment. She explains, "If religious pluralism is promoted here, it is promoted as a social and ethical virtue, the evolutionary product of good democracies, not fundamentally as a theological imperative. This could be perceived as a good thing if the explanation was that the western world accepted Islam on its soil but in fact the western world at least at a popular level was largely indifferent to the Muslims living on its soil."[81]

In response to post-9/11 developments, many writers have sought to foster interaction and open communication between Muslims and non-Muslims to encourage pluralistic attitudes on both sides. In 2005, Husain Kassim of the University of Central Florida called for dialogue between Muslims and other Americans that could lead to the "universalization of norms," based on shared ethical values and not on political expediency, with

Muslims being taken seriously in forging a consensus on common grounds on how to live together.[82] Aware that he is departing from the exegesis of others, he insists that the Qur'an promotes the idea of pluralism in Islam, in the face of the dominant teachings of the Mosque movement, which advocate supersession. He affirms that salvation is available to believers among the People of the Book.[83]

In his first post-9/11 book, *The Place of Tolerance in Islam*, Abou El Fadl shifts his emphasis to the relation of Muslims to non-Muslims. He seeks to dissociate Islam from the Saudi, Wahhabi interpretation promoted by the perpetrators of 9/11. Wahhabi-inspired material was available for American Muslim consumption in books, pamphlets, and magazines. Admitting that there are verses in the Qur'an that are exclusionary, he attempts to put them in context, and as al-Faruqi and Rahman had done, he reaffirms that diversity and difference are the essential teachings of the Qur'an. He notes that while the Qur'an posits claims of absolute truth of the revelation, it does not deny that there might be "other paths to salvation." And since the Qur'an states that there is no compulsion in religion, it is the duty of every Muslim to emphasize the tolerance of Islam, that nonbelievers should not be subjugated.[84]

In 2003 a small number of Muslim scholars, mainly young, gained some prominence for their advocacy of what they called "Progressive Islam."[85] They published a book and set up websites devoted to discussions of an Islam based on concepts of justice, gender equality, and pluralism. They were catapulted into prominence by the media, and for a few months there was an expectation that the proponents of Progressive Islam might become prominent since the government had undermined the established leadership of the Muslim community by raiding their American homes and offices. A book edited by Omid Safi garnered some attention as the authors sought to dissociate Islam from Wahhabi interpretation and rejected any interpretations of Islam that cast it as violent, misogynist, or exclusivist. The book attempted to redefine Islam as governed by justice, including gender and racial justice. While at first it was welcomed as a refreshing new interpretation, it soon receded in popularity among young Muslims as its authors went beyond what is acceptable as Islamic morality, particularly concerning openness to a gay lifestyle.

Several American-born converts to Islam, both African-American (Zaid Shakir, Sherman Jackson, Siraj Wahhaj) and white (Umar Abd-Allah and Hamza Yusuf), have become popular among American Muslim youth. All are bicultural and call on Muslim youth who are alienated from their parents' imported, rigid culture to engage in dialogue with the West while maintaining their commitment to the traditional teachings of Islam. All are engaged in providing instruction in the faith.

Hamza Yusuf, who was born as Mark Hanson in Washington State and converted to Islam in the late 1970s, originally became popular because of his sharp criticism of the United States, declaiming against its decadence, lack of spirituality, and injustice in its foreign policy. After 9/11, he was invited to the White House, where he seems to have undergone a conversion. Rather than focusing on what makes Muslims angry about American policy, he began to focus on the relation between Islam and the West and urged his Muslim listeners to look at the good things in Western society. This transformation in his message has earned him the criticism of the Muslim community, some of whom consider him a collaborator, or even a "pet Muslim."[86] He now regrets his outspoken criticism of American foreign policy in the Middle East as inappropriate and criticized political Islam. "September 11 was a wake-up call for me. I don't want to contribute to the hate in any shape or form. I now regret in the past being silent about what I have heard in the Islamic discourse and being part of that with my own anger."[87]

With Sherman Jackson and Tariq Ramadan,[88] Hamza Yusuf sees a role for American Muslims in fashioning a new interpretation of Islam based on the classical foundation of the faith. He presents Islam as part of the Abrahamic tradition, sharing its values with Christianity and Judaism and not necessarily opposing freedom and democracy. He notes that "it is Islam that has prevented the Islamic world from blowing up in rage—not the opposite."[89]

He is seen as an important link between American culture and Muslim youth who face the travails of integration and assimilation as he attempts to build a bridge between the two. With the other convert rock stars, he embodies the struggle in the search for the meaning of being an American Muslim. He is a white convert who is idealized by nonwhites, for he has rejected the allures of American culture and found fulfillment and meaning in Islam. He now criticizes "Muslim fascists" who peddle a theology of hate. As for Muslims who are critical of the West, he is quoted as saying, "if they are going to rant and rave about the West, they should emigrate to a Muslim country."[90]

In the post-9/11 world, pluralism continues to be a hotly debated and at times divisive topic within the Islamic community. The empowerment of voices that have traditionally been excluded from exerting force in Muslim society, most notably those of racial minorities and women, has become a cause that many emerging Muslim intellectuals have championed. Issues of gender and race have naturally melded with arguments for both inter- and intra-religious pluralism as Muslim thinkers have attempted to guide their listeners toward openness to different religions and to alternative interpretations within Islam.

The promotion of gender pluralism is an emerging cause among many Islamist scholars. In promoting the social and religious voices of Muslim women, Amina Wadud has advocated women's engagement with exegesis of the Qur'an. She notes that there is an absence of women's voices in interpreting the text of the Qur'an and has pointed to the effort to silence women's voices by traditional society. She has called for an alternative exegesis that takes into consideration women's insights in order to foster a holistic Islamic message.[91] Her ideas about "gender jihad" have resonated among Muslim feminists, several of whom began to vocally echo her demand for a women's interpretation of the Qur'an. Another voice calling for gender pluralism is Gwendolyn Zoharah Simmons, who writes, "Frankly, I am tired of the contortions, the bending over backwards, and the justifications for the oppressive, repressive, and exclusionary treatment of women in majority Islamic societies as well as in minority Muslim communities in the U.S.A."[92]

Similarly, many Muslim thinkers are championing racial and cultural equality within Islam. Sherman Jackson calls attention to the fact that immigrant Muslims exclude African-Americans from their deliberations of what Islam is. He warns against commitment to ideologies imported from the Middle East that are exclusionary and do not make room for alternative interpretations. Jackson sees these ideologies as contrary to Islamic tradition, which historically has allowed for competing interpretations that at times are even contradictory. For him, the future of Islam in the United States, particularly after 9/11, is contingent on a pluralistic, nonviolent, tolerant, and egalitarian interpretation of Islam that is inclusive of America and makes room for differences in interpretation. A true pluralistic Islam will have to promote the "collective enterprises of good."[93]

Many thinkers agree that a unified but pluralistic Islam is essential to the prospering of both Muslim and American culture and that differing Islamic ideologies must be allowed for. Mona Siddiqui, for instance, reinforces and elaborates on Jackson's stance, tackling the question of pluralism in the post-9/11 world on a global level:

> The fundamental obligation on us all, then, is to ensure that our societies accept all the challenges of pluralism, religious and secular. For Muslims and Islamic states, this is about remembering that the pluralism on which Islam flourished as a civilization is no longer sufficient for the multiple religious and secular discourses of our contemporary world. The Qur'anic verse, "Had God willed he would have made you all one," must translate into a revisioning of society where Muslim communities can truly accept that religious diversity may possibly be God's will, challenge and blessing on earth. The imperative on us is how we free ourselves from dogmatism and prejudice and be allowed to interpret the Qur'an in such a way that translates meaningfully with human diversity at a local, national and global level.[94]

Umar Faruq Abd-Allah further clarifies the need for a plural Islamic stance in noting that the Prophet and the companions were not at war with the cultures of the world, nor did they try to eradicate ethnicities and fit everyone into a preconceived mold. Furthermore, they did not have a bipolar view of cultures that divided them into good and evil.[95] Building on the growing realization that there are several Islamic cultural zones—as is very apparent in the context of ethnically integrated mosques in the United States that demonstrate that Arab Islamic culture is different from that of Africa, Turkey, Iran, South Asia, and Southeast Asia, and that Chinese Islam is different from all of them—he saw no harm in working to create an American Islam.

For Muzammil Siddiqui, respect for diversity requires recognition of "four important principles: the dignity of the human being, the basic equality of all human beings, universal human rights and fundamental freedom of thought, conscience and belief."[96] He faults the governments of the United States, Canada, and the European Union for not supporting the U.N. Commission on Human Rights, which expresses deep concern about the prevalent stereotyping of religion, particularly Islam, which has been "strongly associated with human-rights violations and with terrorism." He has also expressed concern over the appointment of Bishop J. Delano Ellis as advisor to a congressional panel on faith-based issues. Ellis is noted for his remark about Islam as being "at best false" and at worst "bloody and dangerous."[97]

Conclusion

Most of the writing of Muslim authors on issues of pluralism has focused on the need not only for a *modus vivendi* with American society, but also of developing pluralism in the Muslim community itself. It has emphasized awareness of the great diversity among Muslims, not only in the nationalities they come from but also on issues of race, color, language, and theological and ideological commitments. It calls for tolerance of differences in practice and beliefs among Muslims who adhere to different schools of law, as well as a moratorium on efforts to force people to conform to one school. It looks forward to a future when Muslims will learn to celebrate their internal differences.

Today's Muslims living in the West are in an unprecedented milieu, in that they are living as a religious minority with equal rights granted to the citizens of the state. While some Muslims continue to focus obsessively on the current prevalence of anti-Muslim sentiments and Islamophobia, others have chosen to call attention to the guarantees of the Bill of Rights, which give Muslims the potential to have input into all aspects of the public square, just as other reviled religious minorities of the past, such as Catholics and Jews, have become full constituents of American society.[98] They hold on to the promise of America as a pluralistic society and hope that the day when America will make room for them as Muslims is not far off.

3

The Shaping of a Moderate North American Islam

◉

The events of 9/11 have refocused the preference of American policy makers for "moderate" Islam, a goal that has been promoted by certain sectors in the American establishment since the fall of the Soviet Empire and adopted by President Bush after 9/11.[1] The Bush administration launched several initiatives to foster, nurture, and empower "moderate" Muslims, at the same time that the Justice Department under John Ashcroft promoted legislation and measures that allowed search, seizure, and incarceration of Muslims and Arabs without evidence or recourse to legal advice. This chapter will outline some of the policies and measures implemented since 9/11 by the Bush administration and assess their impact on the American Muslim community, which felt abandoned by a president it supported and helped elect. It will also discuss the pressures from government and political lobbies that are attempting to create a "moderate Islam."

For over a century, Muslims in the United States have lived mostly on the margins of its political life. Several factors have contributed to their marginality: their numbers, their ethnic diversity, and their lack of experience in playing the democratic game. At the same time, other factors and interests in American society have contributed to their exclusion, including the traditional American antipathy toward Arabs and Muslims at least as far back as the founding of the republic[2] and the contemporary political and religious domestic interests of both the pro-Israel lobby and the Christian Right, both of which have managed to keep Arabs and Muslims out of the mainstream. Muslim reluctance to engage in American political activity was finally put aside during the 2000 presidential election when a coalition of Arab-American and Muslim-American political action groups endorsed the Bush-Cheney ticket and contributed financially to the Republican Party.[3] The impetus for their endorsement was the fact that Bush met with the leadership of Arab and Muslim organizations and listened to their concerns, while Al Gore ignored them. Furthermore, during the presidential debates Bush questioned the fairness of the profiling of Arabs and Muslims. Many continue to believe that they provided the margin of difference that delivered the presidency, since they reportedly cast over fifty thousand votes for the Republican ticket. Muslim elation at their success slowly dissipated as they faced the reality of their impotence in reshaping policies defined and pursued by both Republican and Democratic administrations during the last three decades of the twentieth century according to American security and national interests. Upon taking office, the Bush administration shied away from engaging with the Muslim community.

Several events contemporaneous with the increased emigration of Muslims to the United States after 1995 have had a profound impact on Arab and Muslim involvement in the American political process: the 1967 Israeli pre-emptive strike against Egypt, Syria, and Jordan; the Iranian Revolution; the Rushdie affair; and the Gulf War. The Israeli attack and the pro-Israel propaganda in the United States that justified it brought into existence American-Arab organizations eager to improve the negative image of Arabs in America. These organizations identified as Arab and included both Christian and Muslim immigrants from countries including Lebanon, Syria, Palestine, and Egypt.[4] The Gulf War of 1991 energized a new generation of Muslim activists and hastened the appearance of American Muslim organizations seeking to achieve parallel goals under the umbrella of a Muslim identity. Basic to both Muslim and Arab organizations was a confidence in the guarantees of the American Constitution to enable them to voice their views and to create advocacy groups that can inform, correct falsehoods, and seek recourse in the democratic system, in the process negotiating a place for Islam, Arabs, and Muslims in the American mosaic.[5]

As detailed in chapter 1, most of the Muslims who immigrated to the United States came after the repeal of the Asian Exclusion Act in the 1960s. They entered an America that had passed the Civil Rights Act of 1964, the Voting Rights Act of 1965, and the Immigration Act of 1965. It was an America going through an identity crisis, one that was uncomfortable with its racist past, one that had begun to tolerate hyphenated identities. They found the accommodation made by earlier American Muslim citizens to be unacceptable. Casting around for a model of organization for the survival of their identity, they decided to emulate the Jewish community. They noted that although the Jewish community constituted less than 3 percent of the American population, this fact had not impeded its shaping policies and exercising equal power in a society that increasingly defined itself as Judeo-Christian. In the process, they sought equal representation, hoping for a day when the United States would define itself as Christian-Jewish-Muslim. They emphasized difference and distinctiveness as the mark of being Muslim, perceived as a means of ensuring survival of the community and the perpetuation of its faith in the next generation. It became clear that if they would not define themselves, others would continue to define them.

Always latent in American society, prejudice toward citizens of Arab ancestry increased in the 1970s as they were targeted as security risks and held accountable for the acts of individuals overseas. In 1972 the Nixon administration formed a special committee to restrict Arab immigration to the United States, collect data on the immigrants in the United States, and compile dossiers on Arab-American leaders and organizations.[6] By the end of the 1970s, apprehension in the American Arab community intensified when they obtained information through the Freedom of Information Act that the American administration was considering preparing two military compounds in the South for the possible internment of Arabs and Iranians living in the United States.

Early Islamic activism in the West had been related more to circumstances in the countries left behind than to events in America. Some of the immigrants came because they feared persecution on account of their affiliation with Islamic movements. They found the United States hospitable to their goals and were afforded the opportunity to work for opposition groups seeking an Islamic alternative to governments overseas.[7] American interests overseas that promoted Islamization facilitated their activities and encouraged their enthusiasm and eagerness to establish Islamic institutions and foster Islamic states to act as a firewall against the spread of communism.[8] In their annual conventions in the United States, prominent Muslims from overseas were repeatedly invited to address the U.S. Muslim community.[9]

Muslim activists took advantage of the fact that the United States afforded more freedom to think, reflect, organize, publish, and propagate than did the autocratic Muslim nations they had left behind. Once they realized that they were in the West to stay, they started to build permanent institutions to ensure an Islamic future in the United States. They began to envision their role as participants in Western societies, propagators of Islamic values that would help rescue the West from its social degeneration. As events unfolded during the 1980s and 1990s, Muslim activism began to focus more specifically on the American context.

For the Muslim community in the United States, the Gulf War of 1991 brought unexpected consequences. Muslims noted that Arab and Muslim nations joined the coalition against Saddam Hussein, demonstrating their loyalty to the United States and putting to rest the Zionist argument that Israel was "the only reliable American ally in the region." They expected an easing of anti-Arab/anti-Muslim rhetoric in the United States. But the election of Bill Clinton as president of the United States had a negative impact on policies they cherished and hoped to see implemented. Clinton was elected with the support of the pro-Israel lobby, which was eager to punish the first President Bush for threatening to cut off aid to Israel if it did not cease constructing the settlements on the West Bank of the Jordan. At the insistence of Senator Joseph Lieberman, Democrat of Connecticut, Clinton brought twenty-seven activists from the Israeli lobby to formulate and implement his policy vis-à-vis the Middle East. This precipitated a definite shift in American policy toward Islamic nations, dubbed by some as the "Bibi-zation" of American foreign policy, in reference to Bibi Netanyahu's urging Americans to identify Arabs and Muslims as terrorists.[10]

During Clinton's second term, several Muslim states were identified as "rogue states." Even Pakistan, which had been a consistent and reliable ally since the 1950s, was shunted aside in favor of India. All of these events helped foster the growing perception that Islam was the new American enemy, a green menace that had replaced the red menace of the Soviet Union. American Muslims became increasingly aware that their marginalized reality had empowered ideologues who wasted no opportunity to paint Muslims as terrorists and a threat to the United States. Islamophobes such as Steven Emerson, Daniel Pipes, and Bernard Lewis became the goad that spurred Muslims to respond and challenge the veracity of their charges.[11]

At the same time, the Clinton administration, using the politics of symbolic access and inclusion, initiated overtures to the Muslim community that appeared aimed at making Muslims feel included in the political process. In 1993, the Department of Defense commissioned the first Muslim chaplain in the armed forces. This was followed by the appointment of chaplains in all branches of the armed services as well as by the construction of an Islamic prayer hall on a military base in Norfolk, Virginia. The Department of Defense recognized the Graduate School of Islamic Social Sciences as the endorsing agent for the suitability of such chaplains. The administration also appointed the first Muslim ambassador, the first Muslim federal judge, the first Muslim deputy secretary of agriculture, and a Muslim member of the Congressional Commission on International Religious Freedom.

The Clinton administration made other symbolic gestures, such as hosting the first Ramadan *iftar* (breaking the fast) dinners in 1992. Succeeding *iftars* were hosted by the Department of Defense (in 1997) and the Department of State (in 1999 and 2000), and by First Lady Hillary Clinton at the White House in 1996, 1997, 1998, and 1999. In 2000, it was hosted by Bill Clinton since Hillary was running for the Senate from New York and feared Jewish backlash. Robert Seiple, ambassador-at-large for religious freedom, held regular roundtable meetings with leaders of Muslim organizations starting on February 15, 1999, to discuss issues of mutual concern. Even the Postal Service issued a special commemorative *eid* stamp on November 13, 2000.

While some in the Muslim community celebrated inclusion and symbolic access, others were apprehensive about policies simultaneously adopted in the 1990s by various agencies of the federal government that targeted Muslims in the United States, in the process restricting their human and civil rights. These laws were particularly harsh in relation to Arabs and Palestinians. In the aftermath of the Oklahoma City bombing in 1995, media coverage precipitated a backlash against innocent Arab-Americans that led to scores of injuries, incidents of harassment and physical abuse, and attacks on mosques and Islamic institutions. Jingoistic journalists such as Steve Emerson and Connie Chung insisted that the Oklahoma City bombing was the work of Middle Eastern terrorists and had the markings of their *modus operandi*. Although President Clinton appeared on television and warned Americans not to blame or target the Muslim community, Congress passed H.R. 1710, the Antiterrorism and Effective Death Penalty Act of 1995, after the Oklahoma City bombing, and it was signed into law by President Clinton on April 24, 1996. The act gave the American government the right to incarcerate Arab-Americans without evidence. It also sanctioned, among other security measures, airport profiling of potential terrorists. The profile was not of a Timothy McVeigh, the perpetrator of the Oklahoma City bombing, but of an Arab or a Muslim. A further denial of First Amendment rights to noncitizens was sanctioned by a Supreme Court decision in 1999 in the L.A. Eight case against Palestinian Christians and Muslims. Clinton also signed Executive Order No. 12947 on January 23, 1995, which banned contributions to Palestinian charitable institutions by American citizens, depriving orphans, widows, and the needy of American financial assistance. It also allowed for seizing the assets of any American citizen who donated funds to NGOs and civic organizations on the State Department's list of terrorist organizations, including those that supported Palestinian relief agencies such as schools, hospitals, orphanages, libraries, women's organizations, and community centers. In the process, the order curtailed Arab civil liberties and human rights.

President Bush and American Muslims

With the election of the Bush-Cheney ticket, the leadership of the American Muslim community expected better relations with the White House. However, from the start, Muslims noted the absence of even symbolic Muslim participation during the inauguration ceremonies while other religious communities were represented by their leaders. Some in the Muslim political leadership insisted on seeing this as an oversight rather than a snub. When the administration was notified of this absence, it attempted to rectify the situation. A Muslim from Michigan was included at President Bush's announcement of his faith-based voluntary work initiative, which he hoped would be undertaken by churches, synagogues, and mosques. This belated gesture was openly condemned by the Reverend Jerry Falwell, leading some Muslims to expect a presidential condemnation of "hate speech." None was issued. Other Muslims doubted the president's ability to take such an action, given his dependence on the Christian Right. "The administration was only keen in seeking token participation of Muslims without involving them in the decision-making process," one Muslim editorial read.

Another public slight of the Muslim community early in the Bush administration came when the White House announced that it intended to celebrate Eid-ul Adha, to which Muslims were invited. The event was first postponed and finally canceled. When leaders of Muslim organizations asked to meet with the president, their request was ignored. A Muslim journalist wrote in response that the Bush administration "may honor Muslims not as representative of Muslims but as donors to the Republican Party. It may even recruit Muslims to issue statements supporting President Bush. It may even recruit Muslims to join the U.S. propaganda machinery in different parts of the Muslim world. However, it is not serious in appointing Muslims representing the community in positions of significance."[12] (It was not until November 19, 2002, that President Bush invited Muslims to an *iftar* dinner at the White House. While some of the Muslim religious leaders were not invited, ambassadors from Muslim nations were heavily represented, and the event was a grand affair since the dinner was served in the State Dining Room. On November 29, 2002, Secretary of State Colin Powell hosted the American Muslim leaders at the State Department.)

Muslims suspect that the reason President Bush canceled the first *iftar* was his concern about potential criticism for socializing with Muslims. Such criticism would come from the pro-Israel Lobby, which insists on depicting the Muslims as terrorists or as supporting terrorism, or from the Christian Right, which sees Muslims as outside the pale of a Christian or a "Judeo-Christian" state. Seeking to clear the air, the leadership of mainline Muslim organizations asked for and was granted a meeting with the White House. They were about to meet when a security agent came in and escorted out one of the participants, Abdullah al-Arian, claiming that he was a security risk. This happened even though all the participants had been vetted and approved by security agents prior to the meeting and al-Arian was working on the Hill in the office of Congressman David Bonior. Muslim leaders in attendance were offended and walked out of the meeting.

Eventually, the White House arranged a meeting on September 11 to try to patch things up.

By the early part of 2001, some in the Muslim community were beginning to doubt that President Bush was going to act on what they saw as his pre-election promises. While leaders of the Arab and Muslim organizations recognized the constraints under which the Bush administration was operating, they were disappointed by the slow progress in alleviating the harassment of Arabs and Muslims. On May 23, 2001, the American-Arab Anti-Discrimination Committee published an advisory reporting increased frequency during the previous month of passenger profiling of Arab and Muslim Americans at airports. Most disappointing to the group was the fact that the organization had been working with the Department of Transportation and the Federal Aviation Administration since the profiling was instituted in 1996 in the hope of expediting the amelioration of these hardships. The Arab and Muslim community had endorsed George Bush for president precisely because he had voiced concern during the presidential debates about the profiling of Arabs. At the end of August 2001, Muslims were coming to believe that they had achieved numerical parity with the Jewish community in the United States. At the same time, they were increasingly becoming aware that they still lacked clout. The leadership of both Arab and Islamic organizations began to advise patience, warning that politics is the art of the possible. Professor Agha Saeed, who had been instrumental in creating the coalition that made the Muslim voters important players in the last presidential election, outlined the challenges as Muslims continued to attempt political engagement in the United States by exercising their rights as citizens. He noted that Muslims needed "to acquire a better knowledge about the United States, its political institutions and its governance and the means by which consensus is gained," that they should continue to fight all efforts to demonize Muslims and exclude them from participation in the political process, that they should learn how to gain "real access to the political process since symbolic access has not been effective," and that they needed to "earn the right to co-author America's vision of itself and its future."[13] Such calls for political participation proved effective for many immigrant Muslims. A survey of Muslim leadership of mosques issued on April 26, 2001, showed dramatic support (over 70 percent) for the proposition that Muslims should be involved in American institutions and should participate in the political process.[14]

Thus, while the leadership of Muslim organizations continued to be hopeful that Arabs and Muslims could no longer be taken for granted in future elections since their vote could make the difference in critical states, many in their constituency increasingly felt jilted by the Bush-Cheney administration, which had courted them during the campaign. An editorial in a national Muslim publication out of California that had played a major role in building a coalition to support the Bush-Cheney ticket read, "Mr. Bush is no different than other politicians who make promises only to break them, and who will say anything to achieve power in order to serve the agenda of their special interest groups."[15]

A few voices in the American Muslim community were increasingly asking, "What has the Muslim community gained from the Bush-Cheney team? Broken promises and more broken promises."[16] While some hesitated to pass judgment on the policies of the new administration regarding issues of deep concern to Muslims, or on its reluctance to implement meaningful Muslim participation in the political process, others were wondering whether they had been hoodwinked into endorsing Bush for president. The question then was whether the Bush administration had decided that even the politics of symbolic access practiced by the Clinton administration were unpalatable to its supporters in the Christian Right and the watchdog groups of the pro-Israel lobby, which it would need to placate if it harbored any hopes for a second term.

President Bush and American Muslims after 9/11

This policy of ignoring Muslims changed after the catastrophic attack of 9/11, which shattered America's sense of security and self-sufficiency. President Bush visited the Islamic Center in Washington, D.C., in an effort to calm public anger and discourage retribution against Muslims. To the consternation of many of his supporters, he declared Islam a "religion of peace." The government now sought engagement with the Muslim community, but for a price. Not only did it demand the community's repeated denunciation of revolutionary groups overseas, it asked for what Muslims perceived as a rejection of some of the basic tenets of their faith, namely a restructuring of their Islamic organizations and a recasting of their faith as "moderate Islam."

On September 14, 2001, three days after the catastrophic attack on the World Trade Center and the Pentagon, the people of the United States were brought together by President Bush through television in a National Day of Mourning held at the National Cathedral. The event was attended by four former presidents (George H. W. Bush, Bill Clinton, Jimmy Carter, and Gerald Ford) as well as members of the cabinet and Congress and ambassadors of foreign nations. The service was led by religious functionaries of various faith communities. For the Muslims living in fear of backlash from an angry American population, it was a special moment of inclusion. Muzammil Siddiqui, president of the Islamic Society of North America, participated. He prayed,

> We turn to you, our Lord, at this time of pain and grief in our nation. We witness the evil of destruction and the suffering of the many of our people before our eyes. With broken hands and humbled hearts, and with tears in our eyes, we turn to You, our Lord, to give us comfort. . . . Help us in our distress, keep us together as people of diverse faiths, colors and races, keep our country strong for the sake of good and righteousness, and protect us from all evil. Ameen.[17]

Some in the Muslim community were relieved and hailed the inclusion of Muslims by the Bush administration. Others questioned Siddiqui's participation since he stood under a huge suspended cross in the nave of the cathedral. Still others saw him as being used by the Bush administration as a cover in the attempt to project a pluralistic picture to Muslims overseas, at the same time that it initiated a dragnet targeting Muslims and their institutions in an effort to ferret out possible collaborators with the hijackers.

President Bush set the tone of a nation grieving but at the same time determined to combat terrorism and protect itself from further attacks. Bush affirmed, "Our responsibility to history is already clear: to answer these attacks and rid the world of evil. . . . This nation is peaceful, but fierce when stirred to anger. This conflict was begun on the timing and terms of others. It will end in a way, and in an hour of our choosing."[18]

The quest for national security in the aftermath of 9/11 and the desire of the administration not to be caught napping again led to new legislation that made it necessary to initiate new research into the integration and assimilation of Muslims and Islam into the American fabric. To date, scholars have been comparing the immigration and integration of Arabs and Muslims in the United States and their incorporation into the American religious mainstream to that of other ostracized religious groups deemed undesirable by the founding fathers of the republic, such as Mormons, Catholics, and Jews. It is increasingly clear that in the aftermath of 9/11, a more productive comparison might be the experience of the Germans during World War I, the Japanese during World War II, and the communists during the Cold War. The measures adopted by the Bush administration were reminiscent of those taken during critical moments in American history that made it necessary to suspend American legal protection and constitutional guarantees for all citizens and to scrutinize persons identified as a potential threat to the nation.

The attacks of 9/11 appear to have resolved the internal debates among policy makers in the United States that were initiated after the collapse of the Soviet Union, as a growing number of political and religious officials cast around for a new enemy. Some of them had found it convenient to designate "fundamentalist Islam" as the imminent threat, "the other" that needed to be eliminated. Israeli leaders for several decades had been identifying Islam as "the enemy." The attacks of 9/11 revealed a growing consensus among many of the Beltway pundits in Washington, D.C., as well as the press that this was indeed the case. Israel and America were depicted as covictims of Islamic hatred of Judaism and Christianity. The right-wing Christian community had already shifted its interpretation of the signs of the end of times after the Israeli victory of 1967. Included among the signs was now a major battle between Muslims and Jews restored to Israel, a cataclysmic event that would herald the imminent return of the Messiah. Millenarian Christians welcomed the intensification of conflict between the two faiths since it would mean the final redemption of the Jews, and urged Israel to hold firm. Their preachers, casting away all pretense at political correctness, engaged in demonizing Islam and its Prophet with gusto reminiscent of the discourse that launched the Crusades and justified European colonization of Muslim nations.

The events of 9/11 brought further restrictions on the Arab/Muslim community. The Bush administration initiated and Congress passed H.R. 3162, commonly known as USA PATRIOT (Providing Appropriate Tools Required to Intercept and Obstruct Terrorism) Act of October 24, 2001. The Act basically removed all legal protection of liberty for Muslims and Arabs in the United States. It sanctioned, without notification, the monitoring of bank transactions, telephone conversations, e-mail messages, books purchased or borrowed from libraries, credit card purchases, and so on, of any and all individuals, organizations, and institutions deemed suspicious. It has been assessed as violating the Constitution by the American Bar Association, the American Librarians Association, and the American Civil Liberties Union. Former Congresswoman Mary Rose Oakar, president of the American-Arab Anti-Discrimination Committee, argued that it was "completely incompatible with basic civil liberties, most notably freedom from unreasonable search and seizure by the government guaranteed by the Fourth Amendment to the Constitution."[19] Arabs and Muslims have noted that while the Antiterrorism Act had sanctioned the incarceration of Arabs and Muslims with secret evidence, the PATRIOT Act as implemented by Attorney General John Ashcroft sanctioned their incarceration with no evidence. Two hundred and forty-seven cities and towns, including a New York borough a few blocks from Ground Zero, have gone on record rejecting the legislation and its extensive powers to monitor, deport, freeze assets, and incarcerate as violating the Constitution. When several Arab and Muslim organizations and civil rights groups sued the American government, insisting that the PATRIOT Act is un-American, the Supreme Court upheld it, citing the need for security.

The security measures adopted by the Bush administration are perceived both overseas and among many in the Muslim community in North America not as antiterrorism but as anti-Muslim. It appears that these measures reveal a fundamental challenge to the Muslim definition of the role of women in society, which many Muslims deem as prescribed by God in the Qur'an. The Department of State has established bureaus specifically charged with the task of empowering and liberating the women of Islam. It has implemented this charge in a variety of programs, such as funding women's organizations in various Muslim countries, training women from the Middle East and North Africa to participate in the political process, and bringing delegations of women from overseas to learn about women's activities in the United States and about American democracy, pluralism, and tolerance. One delegation of high-powered Arab women included the mayor of a North African city, the vice mayor of a Palestinian town, and a banker from the Gulf. Some in the group expressed indignation at the presumption that they needed empowerment. Their message was that the American government should change its policies to promote economic development in the area rather than create a gender divide. They identified American partiality toward Israel and its failure to condemn Israeli violence as one of the core reasons for Arab anger at the United States. Some even questioned whether the goal of the U.S. government was not in essence to liberate women from Islam and its values.

Another measure adopted by the American administration that has been interpreted as a part of a war on Islam is the monitoring by CIA agents at American embassies overseas of Islamic textbooks for anti-Western, anti-American, or anti-Israeli content. This monitoring has enraged some Muslims, who have accused President Bush of becoming a *mufti*, the arbiter of what true Islam is. At a Christian-Muslim dialogue meeting in Cairo sponsored by the Middle East Christian Council, one of the participants, responsible for the educational programs of the Organization of the Islamic Conference in Sub-Saharan Africa, expressed great concern about the CIA project. "I do not mind if they question my students, my teachers or my principles about what they believe," he said. "But they cannot tell me what Islam is." He expressed willingness to discuss revisions in the curriculum if and when the U.S. government began to censor Jewish educational institutions in Brooklyn that teach hatred of Gentiles and produce gun-toting settlers for the West Bank, as well as Christian institutions such as that in Virginia run by Pat Robertson that teach hatred of Islam and Muslims. While some, persuaded that the United States believes in freedom of religion and speech and would not resort to such action, have dismissed reports about American censorship of school texts as fanciful, there is evidence that such a project is underway. A college professor from Abu Dhabi who was a member of a committee to remove objectionable material from textbooks reported that she was very surprised to find a copy of her report at the American Embassy.[20]

Muslims overseas have not hesitated to express their anger at the Bush administration. Wajih Abu Zikri, writing in *Al-Akhbar*, published in Cairo, reported that President Bush sent personal messages to Islamic scholars, including Shaykh Yusuf al-Qaradawi, asking them to "delete those verses and sayings that Bush sees as 'inappropriate' from the Qur'an." He went on: "President Bush pushed far his crusade, thinking that Islamic education must stop. The Islamic religion should be abolished from all school curricula. The Islamic religion schools should even vanish from the world, and the verses of the holy Koran, that he believes incite the defense of Muslim dignity and respond tit for tat to aggression should be struck out. Bush wants to teach our children to turn the other cheek, and the back to be kicked at will."[21]

Muslims were deeply disturbed by the decision of the Bush administration to monitor NGOs and civic, charitable, and religious organizations, both overseas and in the United States. The government also published a list of suspect organizations whose assets had been frozen. In effect, the American government, in its efforts to curb the transfer of funds to terrorist organizations, was perceived by Muslims to have assumed a veto power over *zakat* (tithing), one of the basic tenets of the Islamic faith, by monitoring charities and organizations that support orphans and widows. Leaders of Islamic organizations met with the administration asking for clarification as to what and who was considered by the American government to be a legitimate recipient of such charities.

Another action by the Bush administration that eroded Muslim confidence that the declared war was really on terrorism and not Islam itself was the raiding by several federal agencies of the homes and offices of the national Muslim leadership in northern Virginia. Muslims saw this as a demonstration by the U.S. government that it was now looking for a new Islamic leadership. The raids came as a major surprise to many Muslims who had previously criticized this leadership precisely because it was cooperating with the American government. Such actions raised serious questions about what kind of Islam America would now tolerate.

American policy makers tend to see the world in polarities, a fact that is evident in war rhetoric and policies engaged in by the Bush administration. The war on terrorism bifurcated the world into good and evil, civilized and uncivilized, democratic versus despotic, free versus held hostage, at the same time insisting on policies that were the antithesis of the American ideals of democracy, tolerance, and civilization that the American elite claimed were the target of the terrorists. In the process, the search for an evil to be vanquished, which had been in process for two decades, appears to have become a dividing line. The United States, while claiming that its goal was the creation of democratic governments in all Muslim nations, was demanding that these same governments demonstrate their Islamic moderation by prosecuting, if not persecuting, suspected terrorists. As Aihwa Ong observed,

"By sharply drawing a line between moderate Muslim leaders and radical Muslim rebels, the US-orchestrated war on terror has increased the power of authoritarian Asian regimes. It has allowed them to brand a spectrum of local opposition or separatist groups as terrorist or al-Qaida-linked. The terrorist discourse is used as a resource against political opponents, to disguise military actions against insurgents at home, and to link sectarian violence at home and terrorism on the global stage."[22]

The Bush administration made it clear that it expected moderate governments to implement other measures to ensure American interests. These included curbing free speech, called "inflammatory" if it was directed against American or Israeli policies. [23] Various administration officials weighed in on how to promote moderate Islam. Paul Wolfowitz, U.S. deputy secretary of defense, said in 2002 at the Brookings Institution Forum that "in winning this larger struggle, it would be a mistake to think that we could be the ones to lead the way. But, we must do what we can to encourage the moderate Muslim voices. This is a debate about Muslim values that must take place among Muslims. But, it makes a difference when we recognize and encourage those who are defending universal values. And, when we give them moral support against the opposition they encounter, we are indeed helping to strengthen the foundations of peace."[24]

Aware of the reaction of Muslims worldwide to its policies and attempting to deal with growing anti-American sentiments, the U.S. government decided that it had failed in public diplomacy, not in policy. In an effort to enhance its image oversees, the Department of State supervised the production of several videos that attempted to demonstrate American pluralism, tolerance, and inclusion of Muslims. The videos featured Muslim Americans touting the freedom they enjoyed in the United States and the fact that their fellow workers appreciated their contributions.[25] Unfortunately, they were aired around the same time the Justice Department was implementing a program that required Muslim males living in the United States to register. The press worldwide was televising the arrest of nearly fourteen thousand males who came to register and were now to be deported; thousands more trekked north and sought asylum in Canada.[26]

The two strongest lobbies in Washington, the Christian Right and the Zionists, had a field day after September 11, 2001. The demonstrated ability of the Muslim community to organize, register voters, and get them out to vote a particular candidate concerned supporters of Israel. "I worry very much from the Jewish point of view that the presence and increased stature, and affluence, and enfranchisement of American Muslims . . . will present true dangers to American Jews."[27] Pro-Israel journalists such as Martin Peretz referred to Muslims in the United States as a "fifth column."[28]

Pro-Israel lobbies have worried and stalked Arab and Muslim activists and organizations for several decades. After 9/11, they swung into action and shared their files with reporters and the media in order to facilitate the investigation of Arab and Muslim individuals and organizations. Solomon Moore reported in the *Los Angeles Times* on November 3, 2002, that such organizations as "the Anti-Defamation League, The Jewish Defense League, [and] the Middle East Forum think tank have provided news organizations with reams of official documentation on Muslim leaders in recent weeks."[29] Pro-Israeli lobbies were instrumental in derailing the nomination of Salam al-Marayati, founder and director of Muslim Public Affairs Council, to the National Commission on Terrorism. His views were exposed by the "Zionist Organizations of America in coalition with the Conference of Presidents of Major American Jewish Organizations, AIPAC, The American Jewish Congress, The American Jewish Committee, and the Anti-Defamation League."[30] They also protested the nomination of his wife, Laila al-Marayati, to the U.S. Commission on International Religious Freedom.

A detailed litmus test of moderate Islam was provided by Daniel Pipes, the presidential appointee to the U.S. Institute of Peace. He is perceived by Muslims as the pro-Israel provocateur who initiated a relentless campaign against "militant/extremist/terrorist Islamists," in the process calling for what could be considered a new Inquisition reminiscent of what obtained in Spain during the fifteenth century. His views on what constitutes "moderate Islam" are notable for their inconsistencies. Many dismiss him as a "designated demonizer," since he set up Campus Watch, which asks students to report on faculty who express ideas that disagree with his orthodoxy. President Bush appointed him to the Institute despite vigorous opposition from the Muslim community, as well as some Christian and Jewish leaders, who saw him as a divider of the nation when what was needed was a healer, and despite opposition to his nomination by scholars and intellectuals as well as senators Ted Kennedy, Christopher Dodd, Tom Harkins, and Jim Jeffords, members of the Senate committee that was reviewing his appointment. Whether Bush's insistence on appointing him during the congressional recess was based on a shared view of "Islamists" or due to the pressure of the pro-Israel lobby is hard to tell.

In an editorial in the *Jewish World Review*, Pipes set out to distinguish between "real and phony moderation," which he asserted cannot be divined by "amateurs like U.S. government officials." He went on to affirm that "the best way to discern moderation is by delving into the record, public and private, Internet and print, domestic and foreign, of an individual or institution. Such research is most productive with intellectuals, activists, and imams, all of whom have a paper trail. With others, who lack a public record, it is necessary to ask questions. These need to be specific, as vague inquiries ('Is Islam a religion of peace?' 'Do you condemn terrorism?') have little value, depending as they do on definitions (of peace, terrorism)."[31]

For Pipes, Muslims need to be questioned regarding their views on a variety of issues, including their attitude toward violence and whether they condone or condemn resistance fighters who "give up their lives to kill enemy civilians." They must condemn by name a list of organizations that he provides. He also challenges the Muslim view of modernity, expecting Muslims to renounce specific teachings of the Qur'an regarding women and the right to resist occupation by foreign troops who expel

Muslims based on religious discrimination, in the process deny-
ing their right to choose and identify their own religion and
culture: "Should Muslim women have equal rights with men
(for example, in inheritance shares or court testimony)? Is jihad,
meaning a form of warfare, acceptable in today's world? Do you
accept the validity of other religions? Do Muslims have anything
to learn from the West?"[32]

Under the rubric of secularism, Pipes asserts that to be considered moderate, Muslims have to renounce certain teachings of
their faith. What is peculiar is that the questions he posits regarding Islamic laws have parallels in Israel, a state he generally defends
as modern, democratic, and secular: "Should non-Muslims enjoy
completely equal civil rights with Muslims? May Muslims convert
to other religions? May Muslim women marry non-Muslim men?
Do you accept the laws of a majority non-Muslim government
and unreservedly pledge allegiance to that government? Should
the state impose religious observance, such as banning food service
during Ramadan? When Islamic customs conflict with secular
laws (e.g., covering the face for drivers' license pictures), which
should give way?"[33]

Pipes is also eager to question Muslims about their understanding of pluralism, whether they consider Sufis and Shi'ites
fully legitimate Muslims (hence admitting to his targeting of
Sunni Muslims). "Do you see Muslims who disagree with you as
having fallen into unbelief? Is takfir (condemning fellow Muslims
one has disagreements with as unbelievers) an acceptable practice?" Furthermore, he provides a category for "self-criticism," in
which he implies that anyone who does not question his or her
faith is not moderate. "Do you accept the legitimacy of scholarly
inquiry into the origins of Islam? Who was responsible for the
9/11 suicide hijackings?"[34]

As for defense against militant Islam, Pipes wants to inter-
rogate Muslims on whether they accept being singled out for
suspicion, profiling, incarceration, or expulsion. "Do you accept
enhanced security measures to fight militant Islam, even if this
means extra scrutiny of yourself (for example, at airline security)?"

He further demands that they acquiesce to measures that impede their right to religious freedom based on accusations without evidence. "Do you agree that institutions accused of funding terrorism should be shut down, or do you see this a symptom of bias?" Finally, he demands that they renounce any missionary activity in the West. "Do you accept that Western countries are majority-Christian and secular or do you seek to transform them into majority-Muslim countries ruled by Islamic law?" That he demands an Inquisition is clear from the text of his opinion piece: "It is ideal if these questions are posed publicly—in the media or in front of an audience—thereby reducing the scope for dissimulation."[35]

To prove that he is not against Islam itself but against extremists, Pipes has provided several other articles that define moderate "Anti-Islamist Muslims—who wish to live modern lives, unencumbered by burqas, fatwas and violent visions of jihad—are on the defensive and atomized. However eloquent, their individual voices cannot compete with the roar of militant Islam's determination, money (much of it from overseas), and violence. As a result, militant Islam, with its West-phobia and goal of world hegemony, dominates Islam in the West and appears to many to be the only kind of Islam." Anti-Islamist Muslims that Pipes approves of include "freethinkers or atheists. Some are conservative, others liberal." Among those on his favored list are Abdelwahab Meddeb of the Sorbonne, "who wrote the evocatively titled *Malady of Islam*, in which he compares militant Islam to Nazism"; Ibn Warraq, a self-described convert from Islam who attempts "to embolden Muslims to question their faith"; and Ayaan Hirsi Ali of the Netherlands, "who has called Islam a 'backward' religion."[36] Others include Irshad Manji, author of *The Trouble with Islam: A Wake-up Call for Honesty and Change*,[37] as well as a slew of journalists and authors, including Saadallah Ghaussy, Hausain Haqqani, Salim Mansur, Khaleel Mohammad, Tashbih Sayyid, Stephen Schwartz, Khalid Duran, and Tahir Aslam Gora. Also on the list of "moderate Muslims" is Shaykh Mohammad Hisham Kabbani, who in a January 1999 address at the Department of State warned against the imminent danger to America from Islamic extremists armed with twenty nuclear bombs. He also warned that 80 percent of mosques in the United States have been taken over by extremists who have an unhealthy focus on the struggle of the Palestinian people.[38] Pipes has also published a list of approved Islamic organizations.[39]

It is clear that the attacks of 9/11 had a major impact on the presidency of George Bush, who declared that they have "changed America forever." The question continues to be whether this change was marked simply by increased vigilance and security measures by Ashcroft's Department of Justice, or if it served as a historical demarcation leading to a permanent shift in American foreign policy. The Muslim world wonders what President Bush meant when he declared, "The battle is now joined on many fronts. We will not waver; we will not tire; we will not falter; and we will not fail. Peace and freedom will prevail."[40] Will this peace include a resolution of the Arab and Israeli conflict such that Palestinians can live in dignity without fear of Israeli repression? Or was President Bush marching to the drum of Pope Urban, who declared a crusade over a millennium ago, or of Napoleon, who invaded Egypt proclaiming that he had come to restore Islam to its genuine teachings?

U.S. Muslim Reactions to 9/11

The initial reaction of the Muslim community to 9/11 was deep shock and fear of potential backlash. Muslims were subsequently surprised and pleased by the response of some in the Christian and Jewish community who supported them. They were grateful to the rabbis and ministers who volunteered to stand guard at mosques, schools, bookstores, and other Islamic institutions to keep avengers away. They were amazed at the number of American women who donned scarves for a day in solidarity with Muslim women who veil. They were also touched by the little gestures of kindness, of neighbors who offered to act as escorts or purchase groceries. They were pleased that Americans were finally interested in Islam and were reading about the religion and getting acquainted with the tenets of their faith.

Profound changes appear to be under way; the ramifications of the attacks are still unfolding. For the majority of Muslims, who emigrated with the idea that if things did not work out they could always return home, the attacks appear to have settled the "myth of return": Muslims are here to stay. The question for them is how to adjust to the intensified scrutiny by anti-immigration groups and government security agencies, which demand repeated public demonstrations of patriotism and allegiance to America and its policies. Many Muslims had a hard time convincing their fellow Americans that because America had been attacked, they felt attacked too. Their repeated denunciations of terrorism as un-Islamic did not seem to be sufficient. Some offered to act as a bridge linking the U.S. government with Muslim organizations overseas and governments in heavily Muslim countries. Others volunteered to serve in the armed services. Thousands volunteered to act as translators, though few were hired due to heightened suspicion of their ethnicity and/or religious affiliation.

That the whole community is under scrutiny has brought about other changes. There is little room for public conflict. There is a new relationship between the mosqued and unmosqued, who had previously disagreed on issues pertaining to integration and assimilation. In the domestic reaction that followed 9/11, exemplified in the policies adopted by the government and the tone assumed by some of the press and some of the evangelical clergy, both groups were targets of hate, of discrimination and profiling, regardless of their religious or political adherence. Sermons in mosques have been restricted to devotional topics. Islamic literature that used to be available for free distribution has disappeared from most public places. Self-censorship has also extended to websites and recommended links.

Another noticeable change is the prominence of Muslim women in the public square. While a few, feeling threatened by a feeling of insecurity and vulnerability, took off the veil to avoid attacks, many put it on. As men began to keep a low profile, the women took charge. Many Muslim women began to assume important positions in the administration of Islamic institutions, as spokespersons and defenders of the community. In this period of tribulation, rather than being delegated to the "sisters" committee, designated as "parallel but equal," women have joined men as "together and equal." They raised funds for the victims of 9/11 and coordinated blood drives for the wounded. They also marched to protest discrimination against Muslims. At the same time, concern over the government policy of incarcerating or deporting males for infractions of the laws has placed some women under duress. In order to safeguard their husbands' and their children's futures, they are reluctant to report domestic problems.

Also noticeable is the fact that the community has embarked on coalition building with human rights, religious rights, and civil rights groups. Relating to non-Muslims has become a priority. They have promoted interfaith occasions, inviting churches and synagogues to come and visit the mosques and engage in dialogue. They have joined national organizations that are seeking justice against corporations and sweatshops, protection of the environment, and peaceful resolution of conflicts. They have begun to seek to build coalitions with civil liberties organizations. Still, many feel that because of their ethnicity or religious affiliation they no longer have the luxury to disagree with government policy. While freedom of thought is a right for all Americans, there seems to be an exception if the Americans are Arab or Muslim. The policy of "You are either with us or against us" appears to allow no room for an independent interpretation of what it means to be Muslim.

Muslims wonder if changing U.S. perceptions of Muslim identity in the wake of the 9/11 attacks are leading to what will amount to a declaration of unrelenting war on the Islamist interpretation of Islam, or whether that war is aiming at undermining mainline Islam. A few individuals have stepped up and volunteered to "lead the Muslims into moderation." Several have been supported and funded by various agencies of the U.S. government. Their mission is to provide new reflections and interpretations of

Islam. They have opened offices and are in the process of leading others into "right thinking." To date, they appear to have few followers, since they are perceived as agents of the effort to undermine Islam. An important collection of essays by several Muslim academics, *Progressive Muslims: On Justice, Gender, and Pluralism*, was published in 2003.[41]

A visiting scholar at the Carnegie Endowment for International Peace, Husain Haqqani, himself a self-proclaimed moderate, urged the United States and other Western powers to revise their definition of what constitutes extremists and moderates in the Muslim world. Rather than considering moderates only as those who "toe the line," he said, moderate Muslims should be defined as those who want to engage as equals with others in the contemporary world and believe that violence, force, and coercion are not appropriate ways in which to respond. Moderate Muslims, he said, are those who "need to be embraced and strengthened."[42]

Conclusion

For over a century, immigrants from the Arab world have prospered in the United States. They have "made it" by working hard, carefully shedding their particular cultural distinctions, compromising, and blending in. They have not, as yet, been welcomed as a group into the American mainstream. The Christians among them who have achieved leadership positions, even as elected governors and senators, mostly abandoned Eastern Christianity, whether Orthodox, Melkite, or Maronite, and joined mainline American churches. Many Muslims question whether the price of belonging in America is contingent on the renunciation of Islam. They are still waiting to be accepted on their own terms into the American definition of its constituent faith communities.

From the outset, officials in various agencies of the American government raised questions about Muslims' fitness to qualify for citizenship in America based on issues of race and color.[43] Spooked by the influx of large groups of immigrants (predominantly from southern and eastern Europe) during the first two decades of the twentieth century, the American public appeared less inclined to welcome Middle Easterners. Helen Hattab Samhan, deputy director of the Arab American Institute, notes that "a judge in South Carolina ruled that Lebanese immigrants even though they may look white, they are not that particular free white person" designated by the 1790 Act of Congress and hence not worthy of citizenship.[44] After a decade of legal debates, the American courts ruled that they qualified as white and were therefore able to become citizens.

In the post–World War II period, when the United States was reinventing itself as a pluralistic society, immigrants from the Arab world found themselves publicly and deliberately excluded from the mainstream of American politics. Helen Hatab Samhan writes about their experience: "In the present period, anti-Arab attitudes and behavior have their roots, not in the traditional motives of structurally excluding a group perceived as inferior, but in politics." She indicates that the political nature of this racism was rooted in the Arab-Israeli conflict, since those who supported the Palestinian cause were subjected to this exclusion whether or not they were Arab-Americans.[45] "It has been not so much Arab origin as Arab political activity in America that has engendered a new form of 'political' racism that takes prejudice and exclusion out of the arena of personal relations into the arena of public information and public policy."[46] This political exclusion was propagated by their political rivals, the American Jewish organizations, who tagged Arab-American activists as an "artificial constituency," a sort of illegitimate group of foreign agents undermining Israel.[47] This eventually brought a variety of government agencies, including the CIA, the INS, the FBI, the IRS, the Department of State, and the United States Customs Service, to coordinate monitoring the Arab-American community in an effort to ferret out terrorists and intimidate the community, weakening its effectiveness and scaring off its allies and sympathizers.[48] Not one instance of a violation of U.S. laws was uncovered.[49] "In the situation of Arab Americans today, exclusion from ethnic politics (i.e., acting as a constituency) is not so much by ignorance or prejudice as by political design. And because Jewish Americans are their main 'adversaries' and can recall their own past victimization (anti-Semitism), the Arab Americans *in their exclusion* often emerge as the villains."[50]

The 1990s witnessed an increase in hostility toward Arabs and Muslims in the United States. The hostile atmosphere appears to have been encouraged by several interests, including the conservative wing of the Republican Party, the religious right, the pro-Israel lobby, and leaders of autocratic Arab states. Events overseas precipitated measures that led to racial profiling and targeting of Arabs and Muslims, along with a growing atmosphere of hostility toward Islam. An act of Congress, a decision of the Supreme Court, and a presidential executive order legitimated the incarceration of Arabs and/or Muslims using secret evidence. In a sense, they were treated as different from other citizens of the United States since they were denied the basic presumption of innocence until proven guilty. Thus, at the beginning of the twenty-first century, the United States, once again, seemed to be questioning whether the members of one group have the same rights as other citizens. This time the discrimination was based not on color or political affiliation, but rather on the perennial fear of the Saracen and the commitment to an Islamic ideology.

Since the 1870s, immigrants from the Arab world to the United States have been engaged in the dialectical process of being and becoming American.[51] This process has been protracted and exacerbated by the new war on terrorism. Each immigrant wave brought its distinctive identity, shaped by events over which it had no control and fashioned by its generation as a response to prevailing conditions and to expectations set up by the governments of the countries from which it came. These identities have also been directly impacted by the vagaries of America's interests, policies, and actions and inactions in the Middle East, as well as the prevailing prejudice toward Arabs and Muslims. Once here, immigrants encounter an America that appears open for a redefinition of its own identity to accommodate the participation of its new citizens, but they experience it as racist and unreceptive to their concerns. America is experienced as having a fluid definition of itself, but at the same time, unwilling to allow the immigrants space to express their equal humanity.

There appears to be a growing tendency in the American media to portray Arabs and Muslims as the consummate "other," as terrorists or, more recently, as the enemy of all cherished Western values.[52] At the same time, some Arabs, surveying the history and experience of the Muslim community worldwide, see themselves as the victims of a virulent anti-Muslim hatred that seeks to subjugate them. They trace this victimization from the Crusades and the *Reconquista* through the age of imperialism, and see it reinforced in contemporary events. Currently, two important factors continue to fashion their identity as they attempt to fit and feel comfortable in the United States: the perception of Arabs and the Arab community in the United States as victims of American and Israeli interests, and the sense that the American environment is not only biased against them, but infused with an endemic prejudice that has been perpetuated in literature,[53] the media,[54] and the movies.[55]

Several events in the late twentieth century appear to have had a profound impact on the formulation of Arab-American and Muslim identity in the United States. Events that heightened Americans' negative perceptions of Arabs, Islam, and Muslims include the Israeli preemptive strike on Egypt, Syria, and Jordan in 1967, the oil boycott of 1973, the Islamic Revolution in Iran in 1979, the Rushdie affair in 1989, and the Gulf Wars. The 1967 war provided the impetus for the formation of American-Arab organizations that sought to ameliorate the negative image of Arabs in America, provide a venue for airing their frustration, and give accurate information. They attempted to redress what they perceived to be one-sided reports about the Arab and Muslim world and sought to exercise their political right to have input into the shaping of policy. The American reaction to the Islamic Revolution in Iran and the anti-Muslim sentiments generated in the American media with headlines such as "America Held Hostage" focused Muslim attention on the unforgiving and sustained rejection of political Islam. It raised questions about American support for

Israel, which defines itself as a Jewish state, and the American rejection of Muslim attempts to create Islamic states.

The Gulf Wars brought to the fore a new generation of Arab and Muslim activists seeking to change American policies by operating within the system. The majority did not approve of the American war on Iraq, not because they were fond of Saddam Hussein or his policies, but because they were not convinced by the government's justification for launching the attacks. They were concerned that the U.S. government did not give diplomacy a chance, since from their perspective it was bent on destroying Iraq's army in order to maintain Israeli domination of the Arab world.

Unlike the activists of the 1970s, the newest generation of Arab-Americans is not spending time on establishing umbrella organizations, writing constitutions for these organizations, or running elections for officials or spokespersons. Rather, it has adopted modern means of communication, including the Internet, to create networks committed to justice and peace. This generation collaborates with existing organizations for human rights, minority rights, and religious rights. These activists are mostly in their twenties and thirties, and they take American values very seriously. They believe that they are working to create a better America, one that is not blinded by special interests but is truly guided by the values it preaches. In the process, they believe that they are truly Arab—and also truly American.

There is a marked difference between those who emigrated in the 1960s and the children and grandchildren of the immigrants of the 1870s. The latter have moved into the middle class and identify as Americans. They and their relatives have been drafted into the American armed forces and have served their country with distinction. One boasted that he had "three times as many relatives [three nephews] serving in the American military, defending American freedom in Iraq as the whole Congress of the United States put together."

The new immigrants who came as adults in the 1960s with preformed identities and a distinctive worldview are in the process of negotiating their identity in a hostile American environment. Increasingly, their children are reshaping them into Americans. For the children, America is the only homeland they know. They often repeat, "I want my parents' religion but not their culture." The parents, on the other hand, have been teaching their Arab culture as Islam, and they want to keep their children within the tradition. It is too early to guess where this process will lead, especially in light of American hostility to nonprivatized Islam. Increasingly, Americans are asking them to define themselves vis-à-vis America. What does it mean to them to be an American? Do they want to be American or hyphenated-American? Do they think of themselves as Muslims living in America? Do they think of themselves as American Muslims? Or do they think of themselves as Americans who happen to be Muslim? While the answers to such questions may vary, there is no doubt that the American public, the American security apparatus, and the American government are increasingly demanding clear and unequivocal answers. In the process, many young people who grew up identifying themselves as American and Muslim are increasingly experiencing relentless prejudice and discrimination. Tempered by prevalent hatred and "othering," many are reidentifying themselves as Arab-American or Muslim-American. As one woman put it, "I feel American, I bleed American, my country denies me that identity because I am a Muslim."

Notes

◉

Chapter 1

1 Daniel Pipes, "The Muslims Are Coming! The Muslims Are Coming!"
National Review, November 19, 1990, 28–31; Martin Kramer, "Islam vs.
Democracy," *Commentary* 95, no. 1 (1993): 35–42.

2 The Christian communities are remnants of early Christian churches.
Among the churches identified as "Orthodox," for example, are those
that follow the Byzantine, Assyrian, Jacobite, Coptic, and Gregorian
rites. Each of these churches has its Catholic Uniate counterpart, those
who have established fealty to the Vatican. More recently, Arab countries
have seen the establishment of new churches representing Protestant
denominations (predominantly Anglican and Presbyterian), along with
smaller Lutheran, Baptist, Jehovah's Witness, Pentecostal, and other
evangelical and sectarian Christian churches. It is estimated that Catholics
(Roman Catholic, Maronite, and Melkite) constitute 42 percent, Orthodox
(Antiochian, Syrian, Greek, and Coptic) 23 percent, and Protestants
(Episcopalians, Baptist and Presbyterian) 12 percent of Christian churches.
"Demographics," Arab American Institute website, http://www.aaiusa.org/
demographics.htm#Religion3.

3 See, e.g., Walter B. Zenner, "The Syrian Jews of Brooklyn," in *A
Community of Many Worlds: Arab Americans in New York City*, ed. Kathleen
Benson and Philip M. Kayal (Syracuse: Syracuse University Press, 2002),

156–69; Dina Dahbany-Miraglia, "American Yemenite Jewish Interethnic Strategies," in *Persistence and Flexibility: Anthropological Perspectives on the American Jewish Experience*, ed. Walter B. Zenner (Albany: State University of New York Press, 1988), 63–78; Sephardic Archives, *The Spirit of Aleppo: Syrian Jewish Immigrant Life in New York, 1890–1939* (Brooklyn, N.Y.: Sephardic Community Center, 1986).

4   It is estimated that 3.4 percent are sub-Saharan African, 2.1 percent European, 1.6 percent white American converts, 1.3 percent Southeast Asian, 1.2 percent Caribbean, 1.1 percent Turkish, 0.7 percent Iranian, and 0.6 percent Hispanic. http://infousa.state.gov/education/overview/muslimlife/demograph.htm.

5   Alixa Neff, *Becoming American: The Early Arab Immigrant Experience* (Carbondale: Southern Illinois University Press, 1985); Elaine Hagopian and Ann Paden, eds., *The Arab-Americans: Studies in Assimilation* (Wilmette, Ill.: Medina University Press International, 1969); Barbara Aswad, *Arabic-Speaking Communities in American Cities* (New York: Center for Migration Studies, 1984); Eric J. Hooglund, ed., *Crossing the Waters: Arabic-Speaking Immigrants in the United States before 1940* (Washington, D.C.: Smithsonian Institution Press, 1987).

6   Kathleen Moore, *Al-Mughtaribun: American Law and the Transformation of Muslim Life in the United States* (Albany: State University of New York Press, 1995); Ian Haney-López, *White by Law: The Legal Construction of Race* (New York: New York University Press, 1996). The famine itself was from 1914 to 1918 and killed about 13% of the population.

7   Salloum A. Mokarzel, "Can We Retain Our Heritage? A Call to Form a Federation of Syrian Societies," *Syrian World* 3, no. 5 (1928): 36–40.

8   Philip Khuri Hitti, *The Syrians in America* (New York: George H. Doran, 1924).

9   Abdo A. Elkholy, *The Arab Moslems in the United States: Religion and Assimilation* (New Haven, Conn.: College and University Press, 1966), 24.

10   Nabeel Abraham, "Detroit's Yemeni Workers," *MERIP Reports* 53 (1977): 3–9; Nabeel Abraham, "National and Local Politics: A Study of Political Conflict in the Yemeni Immigrant Community of Detroit, Michigan" (Ph.D. diss., University of Michigan, 1978).

11   Elkholy, *Arab Moslems*, 15–16.

12   Elkholy, *Arab Moslems*, 18.

13   Elkholy, *Arab Moslems*, 18.

14   Elkholy, *Arab Moslems*, 58.

15   Elkholy, *Arab Moslems*, 34, 37.

16   Elkholy, *Arab Moslems*, 92.

17   Elkholy, *Arab Moslems*, 33, 37.

18   Elkholy, *Arab Moslems*, 33.

19   Elkholy, *Arab Moslems*, 90.

20   Elkholy, *Arab Moslems*, 69, 95, 98.

21   Yvonne Yazbeck Haddad and Adair T. Lummis, *Islamic Values in the United States: A Comparative Study* (New York: Oxford University Press, 1987).

22   Elkholy, *Arab Moslems*, 31–32, 70.

23   Elkholy, *Arab Moslems*, 70.

24   Haddad and Lummis, *Islamic Values*, 126–27.

25   Haddad and Lummis, *Islamic Values*, 132.

26   Haddad and Lummis, *Islamic Values*, 134–36.

27   John V. Tolan, *Saracens: Islam in the Medieval European Imagination* (New York: Columbia University Press, 2002); Norman Daniel, *Islam and the West: The Making of an Image* (Oxford: One World, 1993); V. G. Kiernan, *The Lords of Human Kind: European Attitudes to the Outside World in the Imperial Age* (London: Pelican, 1972); Robert Young, *White Mythologies: Writing History and the West* (London: Routledge, 1990).

28   Karim H. Karim, *Islamic Peril: Media and Global Violence* (Montreal: Black Rose Books, 2000); Edward Said, *Covering Islam: How the Media and the Experts Determine How We See the Rest of the World* (New York: Vantage Books, 1997); Abbas Malek, *News Media and Foreign Relations: A Multi-faceted Perspective* (Norwood, N.J.: Ablex, 1996); William J. Griswald, *The Image of the Middle East in Secondary School Textbooks* (New York: Middle East Studies Association of North America, 1975); Samir Ahmad Jarrar, "Images of the Arabs in United States Secondary School Textbooks" (Ph.D. diss., Florida State University, 1976); Ayad al-Qazzaz, "Images of the Arabs in American Social Science Textbooks," in *Arabs in America: Myths and Realities*, ed. Baha Abu Laban and Faith T. Zeadey (Wilmette, Ill.: Medina University Press International, 1975), 113–31; Glenn Perry, "Treatment of the Middle East in American High School Textbooks," *Journal of Palestine Studies* 4, no. 3 (1975): 46–58.

29   Elaine Hagopian, "Minority Rights in a Nation State: The Nixon Administration's Campaign against Arab-Americans," *Journal of Palestine Studies* 5, nos. 1–2 (1975–1976): 97–114.

30   Michael Palumbo, "Land without a People," 4, Mideastfacts.org website, http://mideastfacts.org/facts/index2.php?option=com_content&do_pdf=1&id=48.

31   Elkholy, *Arab Moslems*, 18.

32   Elkholy, *Arab Moslems*, 48.

33   Elkholy, *Arab Moslems*, 48–49.

34   Helen Hatab Samhan, "Politics and Exclusion: The Arab American Experience," *Journal of Palestine Studies* 16, no. 2 (1987): 16, http://www.jstor.org/stable/2537085; Hatem I. Hussaini, "The Impact of the Arab-Israeli Conflict on Arab Communities in the United States," in *Settler Regimes in Africa and the Arab World: The Illusion of Endurance*, ed. Ibrahim Abu-Lughod and Baha Abu-Laban (Wilmette, Ill.: Medina University Press International, 1974), 201–22; *Near East Report*, May 14, 1969, and October 29, 1969; Hagopian, "Minority Rights," 101.

35 Michael R. Fischbach, "Government Pressure against Arabs in the United States," *Journal of Palestine Studies* 14, no. 3 (1985): 89.

36 For additional details, see Paul Findley, *They Dare Speak Out: People and Institutions Confront Israel's Lobby* (Chicago: Lawrence Hill Books, 1989).

37 Seymour M. Hersh, "A Broad PRogram: Panthers, Saboteur Targets— Hoover Opposed the Plan," New York Times (1923–Current Files), *The New York Times*, May 24, 1973, pp. 1, 34, http://0-proquest.umi.com .library.lausys.georgetown.edu/pqdweb?did=99146877&sid=1&Fmt=10 &clientId=5604&RQT=309&VName=HNP (accessed June 12, 2011); Raphael Rothstein, "Israel: Fighteing Terror With Terror," The Washington Post, Times Herald (1959–1973), *The Washington Post*, October 15, 1972, p. B3. http://0-proquest.umi.com.library.lausys.georgetown.edu/pqdweb ?did=99702836&sid=3&Fmt=10&clientId=5604&RQT=309&VName= HNP (accessed June 12, 2011).

38 Fischbach, "Government Pressure," 87–100.

39 M. C. Bassiouni, ed., The Civil Rights of Arab-Americans: "The Special Measures, information paper #10 (Belmont, Mass.: Association of Arab-American University Graduates, 1974); Hagopian, "Minority Rights," 102.

40 Abdeen Jabara, "The FBI and the Civil Rights of Arab-Americans," *ADC Issues*, no. 5 (n.d.): 1.

41 Jack Shaheen, *Abscam: Arabiaphobia in America* (Washington, D.C.: American-Arab Anti-Discrimination Committee, 1980); Jerry J. Berman, "A Public Policy Report," ACLU Washington Office, October 10, 1982.

42 Ayad al-Qazzaz, "The Arab Lobby: Toward an Arab-American Political Identity," *al-Jadid* 3, no. 14 (1997): 10.

43 Jerome Bakst, "Arabvertising: The New Brand of Arab Propaganda," *Times of Israel*, April 1975, 15–23, as referenced in Hagopian, "Minority Rights," 111.

44 Gregory Orfalea, "Sifting the Ashes: Arab-American Activism during the 1982 Invasion of Lebanon," *Arab Studies Quarterly* 11, nos. 2–3 (1989): 207–26.

45 Khaled Abou El Fadl, "Striking a Balance: Islamic Legal Discourse on Muslim Minorities," in *Muslims on the Americanization Path?*, ed. Yvonne Yazbeck Haddad and John L. Esposito (New York: Oxford University Press, 2000), 52. For more details on the subject, see Khaled Abou El Fadl, "Islamic Law and Muslim Minorities: The Jouristic Discourse on Muslim Minorities from the Second/Eighth to the Eleventh/Seventeenth Centuries," *Islamic Law and Society* 1, no. 2 (1994): 141–87.

46 "Isti'anat al-Muslimin bi'l-Kuffar wa Ahl al-Bid'a wa al-Ahwa'," in *Al-A'mal al-Kamila li'l-Imam Muhammad 'Abdu: al-Kitabat al-Siyasiyya*, ed. Muhammad 'Amara (Cairo: al-Mu'assasa al-'Arabiyya li'l-Dirasat wa'l-Nashr, 1972), 708–15.

47 Abou El Fadl, "Striking a Balance," 52.

48 Sayyid Qutb, *Milestones* (Indianapolis: American Trust, 1990).

49 Syed A. Hassan Ali Nadvi, *Muslims in the West: The Message and Mission* (London: Islamic Foundation, 1983), 111.

50 Nadvi, *Muslims in the West*, 158.

51 Muhammad Ali Kettani, *Muslim Minorities in the World Today* (London: Mansell, 1986), 9–13. For further discussion on the topic, see Yvonne Yazbeck Haddad, "The Challenge of Muslim Minorityness: The American Experience," in *The Integration of Islam and Hinduism in Western Europe*, ed. W. A. R. Shadid and P. S. van Koningsveld (Kampen: Kok Pharos, 1991), 134–53.

52 Barbara Daly Metcalf, "New Medinas: The Tablighi Jama'at in America and Europe," in *Making Muslim Space in North America and Europe*, ed. Barbara Daly Metcalf (Berkeley: University of California Press, 1996), 110–27.

53 Muhammad Abdul-Rauf, "The Future of the Islamic Tradition in North America," in *The Muslim Community in North America*, ed. Earle H. Waugh, Baha Abu-Laban, and Regula B. Qureshi (Edmonton: University of Alberta Press, 1983), 271–72.

54 Mohammad T. Mehdi, *Of Lions Chained: An Arab Looks at America* (San Francisco: New World Press, [1962]).

55 Mohammad T. Mehdi, *Terrorism: Why America Is the Target* (New York: New World Press, 1988).

56 Mohammad T. Mehdi, *Peace in Palestine* (New York: New World Press, 1976).

57 See John L. Esposito, "Ismail R. Al-Faruqi: Muslim Scholar-Activist," in *The Muslims of America*, ed. Yvonne Yazbeck Haddad (New York: Oxford University Press, 1991), 65–79.

58 For his ideas on Arabism, see Ismail Raji al-Faruqi, *On Arabism: Urubah and Religion* (Amsterdam: Djambatan, 1962).

59 As quoted in M. Tareq Quraishi, *Ismail al-Faruqi: An Enduring Legacy* (Plainfield, Ind.: Muslim Student Association, 1987), ii.

60 Ismail Raji al-Faruqi, *Tawhid: Its Implications for Thought and Life* (Kuala Lumpur: International Institute of Islamic Thought, 1982).

61 K. Ahmed, Arne Rudvin, et al., *Christian Mission and Islamic Da'wah: Proceedings of the Chambesy Dialogue Consultation* (Leicester: Islamic Foundation, 1982).

62 Ismail Raji al-Faruqi, *Trialogue of the Abrahamic Faiths* (Herndon, Va.: International Institute of Islamic Thought, 1986).

63 Ismail Raji al-Faruqi, *Islam and Culture* (Kuala Lumpur: ABIM, 1980).

64 Conversation with the author in 1982.

65 Mohamad Fathi Osman, "Towards a Vision and an Agenda for the Future of Muslim Ummah," in *Islam: A Contemporary Perspective*, ed. Muhammad Ahmadullah Siddiqui (Chicago: NAAMPS, 1994), 13–22.

66 Maher Hathout, "Islamic Work in North America: Challenges and Opportunities," in Muhammad Ahmadulla Siddiqui, *Islam*, 13.

67   Salam al-Marayati, "Formulating an Agenda of Political Actions for North American Muslims," in Muhammad Ahmadulla Siddiqui, *Islam*, 64–69.

68   Al-Marayati, "Formulating an Agenda," 70.

Chapter 2

1   George W. Bush, "Remarks by the President at Islamic Center of Washington, D.C.," accessed September 22, 2005, http://georgewbush -whitehouse.archives.gov/news/releases/2001/09/20010917-11.html.

2   Muzammil Siddiqui, "Unity and Diversity: Islamic Perspective," 1, accessed June 3, 2007, http://www.theamericanmuslim.org/tam.php/ features/articles/unity_and_diversity_islamic_perspective/.

3   The alternative term coined for privatization is *takhsis*. 'Abd al-Rahman al-Rashid, "Bay' al-I'lam al-'Arabi," *al-Majalla*, no. 707 (August 14–20, 1994): 13.

4   Jabir Sa'id 'Awad, "Mafhum al-Ta'addudiyya fi al-Adabiyyat al-Mu'asira: Muraja'a Naqdiyya," in *Nadwat al-Ta'addudiyya al-Hizbiyya wa al-Ta'ifiyya wa al-'Irqiyya fi al-'Alam al-'Arabi* (Herndon, Va.: International Institute of Islamic Thought, 1993), 2.

5   Ismail Raji al-Faruqi, "Common Bases between the Two Religions in Regard to Convictions and Points of Agreement in the Spheres of Life," in *Seminar of the Islamic-Christian Dialogue* (Tripoli: Republic Office of Foreign Relations, Socialist Peoples Libyan Arab Jamahiriya, 1981), 229–64.

6   Muhammad 'Abduh, *Al-A'mal al-Kamila*, tahqiq wa-taqdim Mohammad 'Imara (Cairo: Dar al-Shuruq, 1993), 3:291–92.

7   Abduh, *Al-A'mal*, 3:290.

8   'A'isha 'Abd al-Rahman, *Al-Isra'iliyyat fi al-Ghazu al-Fikri* ([Cairo], 1975); Anwar al-Jindi, *Afaq Jadadah fi al-Adab wa-al-Tarikh wa-al-Tarajum* ([Cairo]: Maktaat al-Anjulu al-Misriyah, [1978]), 20–22; Salim 'Ali al-Bahnasawi, *Al-Ghazu al-Fikri li al-Tarikh wa al-Sira bayn al-Yamin wa al-Yasar* (Kuwait, 1985), 111–47; 'Ali 'Abd al-Halim Mahmud, *Al-Ghazu al-Fikri wa al-Tayyarat al-Mu'adiya li al-Islam* (Riyad, 1984); Hassan Muhammad Hassan, *Wasa'il Muqawamat al-Ghazu al-Fikri li-al-'Alam al-Islami* (Mecca, [1981]); 'Ali 'Abd al-Halim Mahmud, *Al-Ghazu al-Fikri wa-Atharuhu fi al-Mujtama' al-Islami al-Mu'asir* (Kuwait, 1979); 'Ali Muhammad Jarisha and Muhammad Sharif al-Zaybaq, *Asalib al-Ghazu al-Fikri li-al-'Alam al-Islami* (Cairo, [1977]); Muhammad Faraj, *Al-Islam fi Mu'tarak al-Sira' al-Fikri al-Hadith* (Cairo, 1962); Muhammad Jalal Kishk, *Al-Ghazu al-Fikri* (Cairo, 1975).

9   The early students who went to Europe were grounded in their own culture: "there was no room for western thought to invade their personality and distort their identity." Under colonialism, the door was opened for missionary schools and foreign educational institutions from every race,

religion, and language. "They received our young, impressionable children and promised to educate them, enculturate them, and guide them, to fashion them as strangers in their own lands in language, thought, and consciousness. They were freed from the complex of disdain for the European, which was replaced with an inferiority complex toward westerners due to the long insistence of the soldiers of the secular and [Christian] missionaries on their conscience and intellect that Eastern is a symbol for retardation and backwardness, Arabic language is the source of underdevelopment and disease, while Islam is the image of ossification and sterility." 'Abd al-Rahman, *Al-Isra'iliyyat*, 58–59.

10 Sayyid Qutb, *Fi Zilal al-Qur'an*, 6 vols. (Beirut, 1980), 2:816.

11 Qutb, *Fi Zilal*, 2:828.

12 Qutb, *Fi Zilal*, 2:829.

13 Qutb, *Fi Zilal*, 2:874.

14 Qutb, *Fi Zilal*, 3:1564. For further reflection on the issue, see Fahmi Huwaydi, *Li'l-Islam Dimuqratiyya* (Cairo, 1993), 32–34.

15 Qutb, *Fi Zilal*, 2:908.

16 Qutb, *Fi Zilal*, 2:910.

17 Qutb, *Fi Zilal*, 2:915.

18 Qutb, *Fi Zilal*, 3:1620.

19 Qutb, *Fi Zilal*, 3:1633.

20 Mohammed Arkoun, *Al-Hawamil Wa-al-shawamil: hawl Al-Islam Al-mus'asir* (Beirut: Dar al-Tali'ah, 2010), 16.

21 Ahmad al-Shuqayri, *al'A'mal al-kamilah*; taqdim Anis Sayigh; tahrir Khayriyah Qasimiyah (Beirut: Markaz Dirasat al-Wahdah al-'Arbiyah, 2006), 20.

22 Rajab Madkur, *Al-Takfir wa al-Hijra Wajhan li-Wajh* (Cairo, 1985); Nu'man 'Abd al-Raziq al-Samirra'i, *Al-Takfir: Judhuruh-Asbabuh-Mubarriratuh* (Jiddah, 1984); Salim 'Ali al-Bahnasawi, *Al-Hukm wa Qadiyyat Takfir al-Muslim* (Kuwait, 1985); Hassan al-Hudaybi, *Du'at la Qudat* (Beirut, 1978); Yusuf al-Qaradawi, *Al-Sahwa al-Islamiyya bayn al-Juhud wa al-Tatarruf*, Kitab al-Umma 4 (Doha, Qatar, 1985); Yusuf al-Qaradawi, *Zahirat al-Ghuluww fi al-Takfir* (Kuwait, 1985); Muhammad 'Abd al-Hakim Hamid, *Zahirat al-Ghuluww fi al-Din fi al-'Asr al-Hadith* (Cairo, 1991).

23 Yusuf al-Qaradawi, *Ghayr al-Muslimin fi al-Mujtama' al-Islami* (Beirut, 1983).

24 Al-Qaradawi, *Ghayr al-Muslimin*, 7–12.

25 Al-Qaradawi, *Ghayr al-Muslimin*, 49.

26 Al-Qaradawi, *Ghayr al-Muslimin*, 20–23, 41.

27 Al-Qaradawi, *Ghayr al-Muslimin*, 80–81.

28 Qutb's most radical ideas were published in his *Milestones* and his commentary on the Qur'an, *Fi Zilal al-Qur'an*. Cf. "Sayyid Qutb: Ideologue of Islamic Revival," in Esposito, ed., *Voices of Resurgent Islam*, 67–98; Yvonne

Yazbeck Haddad, "The Qur'anic Justification for an Islamic Revolution," *Middle East Journal* 37, no. 1 (1982): 14–29.

29   For a discussion of his life and work, see Charles J. Adams, "Mawdudi and the Islamic State," in Esposito, ed., *Voices of Resurgent Islam*, 99–133; cf. K. Ahmad and Z. I. Ansari, eds., *Islamic Perspectives: Studies in Honour of Sayyid Abul A'la al-Mawdudi* (Leicester: Islamic Foundation, 1979).

30   Zaki Ahmad, "Al-Ta'addudiyya al-Hizbiyya fi al-Fikr al-Islami al-Mu'asir," in *Nadwat al-Ta'addudiyya al-Hizbiyya*, 1.

31   The symposium took place in Amman, Jordan, October 25–27, 1986, and the proceedings were published in *Majallat al-Ufuq al-'Arabi*, no. 9 (1987).

32   The Symposium on Political Pluralism in the Arab World was sponsored by the Center for Arab Unity in Amman, Jordan, March 26–28, 1989. The proceedings were published in *Muntada al-Fikr al-'Arabi*.

33   Mustafa Mashhur, "Al-Ta'addudiyya al-Hizbiyya," *Al-Sha'b*, October 4, 1993; Salah al-Sawi, *Al-Ta'addudiyya al-Siyasiyya fi al-Islam* (Cairo, 1992).

34   The proceedings were published in *Majallat Minbar al-Sharq* 1 (1992).

35   Muhyi al-Din 'Atiyyah, "Al-Ta'addudiyya: Qa'ima Biblioghrafiyya Intaqat," in *Nadwat al-Ta'addudiyya al-Hizbiyya*. The bibliography included the papers delivered at a symposium on Pluralism in Political Parties, Sects, and Race in the Arab World sponsored by the International Institute of Islamic Thought in Herndon, Virginia, November 26–December 1, 1993.

36   For a study of reflections on the role of Christians in an Islamic state, see Yvonne Yazbeck Haddad, "Christians in a Muslim State: The Current Egyptian Debate," in *Christian-Muslim Encounters*, ed. Yvonne Yazbeck Haddad and Wadi Zaidan Haddad (Gainesville: University Press of Florida, 1995). Cf. 'Abd al-malik Salman, "Al-Tasamuh Tijah al-Aqalliyyat Kadarura li al-Nahda," in *Nadwat al-Ta'addudiyya al-Hizbiyya*.

37   Ahmad, "Al-Ta'addudiyya," 1.

38   Muhammad Salim al-'Awwa, *Fi al-Nizam al-Siyasi li al-Dawla al-Islamiya* (Cairo: Dar Al-Shuruq, 1989), 12.

39   Fahmi Huwaydi, *Muwatinun la Dhumiyyun: Mawqi' Ghayr al-Muslimin fi Mujtama' al-Muslimin* (Beirut, 1985).

40   S. 5:69, 109:6, 5:48, 6:35, 10:99.

41   Huwaydi, *Muwatinun*, 225.

42   Muhammad 'Amara, ed., "Al-Ta'addudiyya: al-Ru'ya al-Islamiyya wa al-Tahadiyat al-Gharbiyya," in *Nadwat al-Ta'addudiyya al-Hizbiyya*, 3–14.

43   Abduh, *Al-A'mal*, 3:283.

44   See, e.g., S. 6:98-99 35:27-28, 30:22, 49:13. Ahmad, "Al-Ta'addudiyya," 6. Cf. Sa'd al-Din Ibrahim, *Al-Ta'addudiyya al-Siyasiyya wa al-Dimuqratiyya fi al-Watan al-'Arabi* (Amman, 1989), proceedings of a conference held March 26–28, 1989.

45   Huwaydi, *Li'l-Islam*, 22.

46   Ismail Raji al-Faruqi, "The Role of Islam in Global Inter-Religious Dependence," in al-Faruqi, *Islam and Other Faiths*, 72. Originally printed

in *The Challenge of Islam*, ed. A. Gauhar (London: Islamic Council of Europe, 1978), 82–111. Reprinted in *Towards a Global Congress of the World's Religions*, ed. Warren Lewis (Barrytown, N.Y.: Unification Theological Seminary, 1980), 19–38. Hereinafter cited as *Islam and Other Faiths*.

47 Al-Faruqi, "The Role of Islam," 74–75.

48 Al-Faruqi, "The Role of Islam," 91–92.

49 Al-Faruqi, "The Role of Islam," 140.

50 Al-Faruqi, "Islam and Other Faiths." Reprinted in al-Faruqi, *Islam and Other Faiths*, 138.

51 Ismail Raji al-Faruqi, "Islam and Christianity: Diatribe or Dialogue," *Journal of Ecumenical Studies* 5 (1968): 45–77. Reprinted in al-Faruqi, *Islam and Other Faiths*, 269.

52 Al-Faruqi, "Islam and Other Faiths," 151.

53 Al-Faruqi, "The Role of Islam," 72.

54 Al-Faruqi, "The Role of Islam," 103.

55 Fazlur Rahman, *Major Themes of the Qur'an* (Minneapolis: Bibliographica Islamica, 1980, 165–66).

56 Rahman, *Major Themes of the Qur'an*, 166–67.

57 Rahman, *Major Themes of the Qur'an*, 167.

58 Samuel P. Huntington, "The Clash of Civilizations?" *Foreign Affairs* 72 (1993): 22–49.

59 Mohamed Fathi Osman, *The Children of Adam: An Islamic Perspective on Pluralism* (Washington, D.C.: Center for Muslim Christian Understanding, 1996), 13.

60 Osman, *The Children of Adam*, 31.

61 Abdulaziz Sachedina, *The Islamic Roots of Democratic Pluralism* (New York: Oxford University Press, 2001), 139.

62 Abdulaziz Sachedina, *The Qur'an on Religious Pluralism*, Occasional Paper Series (Washington, D.C.: Center for Muslim-Christian Understanding), 11.

63 Sachedina, *The Qur'an*, 13.

64 Sachedina, *The Qur'an*, 16.

65 Sachedina, *The Qur'an*, 19.

66 Sachedina, *The Islamic Roots*, 11–14.

67 Khalid Abou El Fadl, *The Authoritative and the Authoritarian in Islamic Discourse: A Contemporary Case Study* (Dar Taiba, 1997), 16.

68 Sulayman S. Nyang, "Seeking the Religious Roots of Pluralism in the United States of America: An American Muslim Perspective," *Journal of Ecumenical Studies* 34, no. 3 (1997): 402–17.

69 Nyang, "Seeking the Religious Roots of Pluralism."

70 Nyang, "Seeking the Religious Roots of Pluralism."

71 Farid Esack, *Qur'an, Liberation and Pluralism* (Oxford: One World, 1997), 78.

72   Esack, *Qur'an, Liberation and Pluralism*, 179.
73   Mahmoud Mohamed Taha, *The Second Message of Islam*, trans. Abdullahi A. An-Na'im (Syracuse: Syracuse University Press, 1987).
74   Taha, *The Second Message*, 17.
75   Abdullahi A. An-Na'im, "Religious Minorities under Islamic Law and the Limits of Cultural Relativism," *Human Rights Quarterly* 9 (1987): 10.
76   Taha, *The Second Message*, 11.
77   An-Na'im, "Religious Minorities," 10–11.
78   M. A. Muqtedar Khan, "Living on Borderlines: Beyond the Clash of Dialogue," in *Muslims' Place in the American Public Square*, ed. Zahid H. Bukhari, Sulayman S. Nyang, Mumtaz Ahmad, and John L. Esposito (Walnut Creek, Calif.: AltaMira Press, 2004), 90–93.
79   Edward P. Djerejian, "The United States and the Middle East in a Changing World: Diversity, Interaction and Common Aspirations," policy paper delivered at Meridian House and at the Middle East Institute's 46th Annual Conference, October 16, 1992. http://www.disam.dsca.mil/pubs/Vol%2014_4/Djerejian.pdf. Cf. Yvonne Yazbeck Haddad, "The 'New Enemy'? Islam and Islamists after the Cold War," in *Altered States: A Reader in the New World Order*, ed. Phyllis Bennis and Michel Moushabeck (New York: Olive Branch Press, 1993), 83–94.
80   Mona Siddiqui, "Islam: Issues of Political Authority and Pluralism," *Political Theology* 7, no. 3 (2006): 338.
81   Mona Siddiqui, "Islam," 339.
82   Husain Kassim, *Legitimizing Modernity in Islam: Muslim Modus Vivendi and Western Modernity* (Lewiston, Maine: Edwin Mellen Press, 2005), 138–46.
83   See Yvonne Yazbeck Haddad, "Islamist Depictions of Christianity in the Twentieth Century," *Islam and Christian Muslim Relations* 11, no. 3 (2000): 75–94.
84   Khalid Abou El Fadl, *The Place of Tolerance in Islam* (Boston: Beacon Press, 2002), 17.
85   Omid Safi, *Progressive Muslims: On Justice, Gender and Pluralism* (Oxford: One World, 2003).
86   Jack O'Sullivan, "If You Hate the West, Emigrate to a Muslim Country," *Guardian*, October 8, 2001, features pages, 4.
87   O'Sullivan, "If You Hate the West."
88   Sherman A. Jackson, *Islam and the Black American: Looking toward the Third Resurrection* (New York: Oxford University Press, 2005); Tariq Ramadan, *Western Muslims and the Future of Islam* (New York: Oxford University Press, 2003).
89   Don Lattin, "North American Muslims Ponder Effect of 9/11 on Them," *San Francisco Chronicle*, September 2, 2002, A3.
90   O'Sullivan, "If You Hate the West."

91   Amina Wadud, "Alternative Qur'anic Interpretation and the Status of Women," in *Windows of Faith: Muslim Women Scholar-Activists in North America*, ed. Gisela Webb (Syracuse: Syracuse University Press, 2000), 3–21; see also Amina Wadud, *Inside the Gender Jihad: Women's Reform in Islam* (London: One World, 2006).

92   Gwendolyn Zoharah Simmons, "Are We Up to the Challenge? The Need for a Radical Reordering of the Discourse on Women," in Safi, *Progressive Muslims*, 235.

93   Sherman A. Jackson, "Islam(s) East and West: Pluralism between No-Frills and Designer Fundamentalism," in *September 11 in History: A Watershed Moment?* ed. Mary L. Dudziak (Durham: Duke University Press, 2003), 112–35.

94   Mona Siddiqui, "Islam," 348.

95   Umar Faruq Abd-Allah, "Islam and the Cultural Imperative," Foundation Paper, Nawawi Foundation (Burr Ridge, Ill., 2004), 4.

96   Muzammil Siddiqui, "Unity and Diversity," 3.

97   Muzammil Siddiqui, "Unity and Diversity," 4.

98   Nyang, "Seeking the Religious Roots of Pluralism."

Chapter 3

1   Special thanks to my research assistants, Nicholas Reith and Ahmed Humayun, for their help in locating and compiling information for this chapter. This chapter is reprinted by permission of the publishers of "The Shaping of a Moderate North American Islam: Between 'Mufti' Bush and 'Ayatollah' Ashcroft," in *Islam and the West Post-9/11*, ed. Ron Geaves, Theodore Gabriel, Yvonne Haddad, and Jane Idleman Smith (Farnham, U.K.: Ashgate, 2004), 97–115. © 2004.

2   See, e.g., Timothy Worthington Marr, "Imagining Orientalism in America from the Puritans to Melville" (Ph.D. diss., Yale University, 1997); Marwan M. Obeidat, "The Muslim East in American Literature: The Formation of an Image" (Ph.D. diss., Indiana University, 1985).

3   The American Muslim Political Coordinating Council (AMPCC) was formed as an umbrella organization representing the American Muslim Alliance, the American Muslim Council, the Council on American-Islamic Relations, and the American Public Affairs Council.

4   These organizations include the following: (1) The Association of Arab-America University Graduates (AAUG), founded in 1967 by professionals, university professors, lawyers, doctors, and many veterans of the Organization of Arab Students (OAS). (2) The National Association of Arab-Americans (NAAA), organized in 1972 and modeled after the pro-Israeli lobby the American Israel Public Affairs Committee. Its leadership seeks to meet with members of congress educate Arab Americans on the political process. (3) The American-Arab Anti-Discrimination Committee

(ADC), founded in 1980 by former senator from South Dakota James Aburezk. Modeled after the ADL, its purpose is to fight racism, prejudice and discrimination against Arabs. It is currently the largest Arab-American grassroots organization, with chapters throughout the United States. (4) The Arab American Institute (AAI), established in 1984 when Jim Zogby split with Aburezk. It encourages participation in the political system and seeks to get Arab-Americans to run for office. It has established Democratic and Republican clubs and was active in Jesse Jackson's run for office in 1988. These organizations are discussed further in chapter 1.

5   They include the following: (1) The American Muslim Alliance (AMA), which focuses on voter registration, political education, and leadership training and seeks Muslim participation as voters and elected officials nationwide in both parties. (2) The American Muslim Council (AMC), established in 1990 with a focus on increasing Muslim participation in the political process. It gained legitimacy by arranging for Muslim religious leaders to open the House of Representatives with a Muslim invocation, hosted hospitality suites at the Democratic and Republican party conventions in 1992 and 1996, and worked for a more balanced Freedom from Religious Persecution Act and for the repeal of "secret evidence." (3) American Muslims for Global Peace and Justice (Global Peace), established in 1998, which focuses on creating networks working for human dignity, freedom, peace, and justice. (4) American Muslims for Jerusalem (AMJ), incorporated in 1999, which works to present accurate information about Muslim concerns about Jerusalem. (5) The Council on American-Islamic Relations (CAIR), established in 1994 to promote a positive image about Islam and Muslims and to seek to empower Muslims in America through political and social activism. (6) The Muslim American Society (MAS), founded in 1992 by the ministry of Warith D. Mohammed to promote a better society. It has a political arm, Muslims for Better Government, that is involved in voter registration and political education. (7) The Islamic Institute, founded in 1998 to create a better understanding between the Muslim community and the political leadership. (8) The Muslim Public Affairs Council (MPAC), which is involved in political activism. The AMA, AMC, and CAIR are discussed further in chapter 1.

6   al-Qazzaz, "The Arab Lobby," 10.

7   Omar Afzal, "Learn Not Copy: Movements Facing Challenges of the West," *Message*, March 1996, 23.

8   Afzal, "Learn Not Copy," 23.

9   Afzal, "Learn Not Copy," 23.

10 Netanyahu's publications include Binyamin Netanyahu, ed., *International Terrorism, Challenge and Response: Proceedings of the Jerusalem Conference on International Terrorism* (New Brunswick, N.J.: Transaction Books, 1981); *Terrorism: How the West Can Win* (New York: Farrar, Straus & Giroux,

1986); *Fighting Terrorism: How Democracies Can Defeat Domestic and International Terrorism* (New York: Farrar, Straus & Giroux, 1995).

11 Among the most vociferous is Steven Emerson, who produced the controversial documentary *Jihad in America*, aired on PBS, in which he claimed that Muslims use mosques for terrorist training. He also appeared before the House International Committee, where he asserted that "radical Islamic networks now constitute the primary domestic—as well as international—national security threat facing the FBI and other law enforcement agencies." Steven Emerson, "Testimony of Steven Emerson: Subcommittee of Africa House International Relations Committee," U.S. House of Representatives, April 6, 1995, 4. He was one of the first journalists to ascribe the Oklahoma City bombing to Muslim terrorists, as vindication of his analysis and assessment. He has also published an article ("The Other Fundamentalists," *New Republic*, June 12, 1995, 21–30) and has written a book on the topic (*American Jihad: The Terrorists Living Among Us* [New York: The Free Press, 2002]).

12 "Has the Bush Administration Benefitted Muslim Americans?" *Minaret* 23, no. 5 (2001): 7.

13 Agha Saeed, "The American Muslim Paradox," in *Muslim Minorities in the West: Visible and Invisible*, ed. Yvonne Yazbeck Haddad and Jane I. Smith (Walnut Creek, Calif.: AltaMira Press, 2002), 39–58.

14 Ihsan Bagby, Paul M. Pearl, and Bryan T. Froehle, "The Mosque in America: A National Portrait," released by the Council on American-Islamic Relations, Washington, D.C., April 26, 2001, 4.

15 "Has the Bush Administration?" 10.

16 "Has the Bush Administration?" 7.

17 Ayesha Ahmad and Neveen A. Salem, "Faiths Come Together at National Cathedral on National Day of Mourning," Islam On Line, accessed January 31, 2004.

18 "President's Remarks at National Day of Prayer," http://georgebush -whitehouse.archives.gov/news/releases/2001/09/20010914-2.html.

19 Other Arab-American and Islamic organizations that joined ADC in the brief include the Muslim Community Association of Ann Arbor, the Arab Community Center for Economic and Social Services, Bridge Refugee and Sponsorship Services, the Council on American and Islamic Relations, and the Islamic Center of Portland and Masjid as-Saber, Portland, Oregon.

20 Interview with Fatima Al-Saawegh.

21 Wajih Abu Zikri, "A New American Religion for Muslims," *al-Akhbar*, December 26, 2001. FIBIS-NES-2001-1226.

22 Aihwa Ong, "A Multitude of Spaces: Radical versus Moderate Islam," paper presented at the AAA annual meeting in New Orleans, November 21, 2002. http://www.anthropology.emory.edu/FACULTY/ANTBK/files/ AAA%20Ong%20Revised.PDF.

23 Farish A. Noor, "The Other Malaysia: Panopticon Revisited," November 6, 2002, Malaysikini.org website. http://www.malaysiakini.com/columns/20634.

24 Paul Wolfowitz, remarks at a Brookings Institution Issues Forum, September 5, 2002, http://www.brookings.edu/comm/events/20020905 .pdf, pp. 3–13.

25 Jane Perlez, "Muslim-as-Apple-Pie Videos Are Greeted with Skepticism," *The New York Times*, October 30, 2002.

26 See, e.g., Mae E. Cheng, "Legal Catch-22 for Immigrants," *Newsday*, December 14, 2003.

27 Daniel Pipes, as quoted in Dave Eberhart, "Muslim Moderate Kabbani Firm on Terrorist Nuclear Threat," Newsmax.com, November 19, 2001. http://archive.newsmax.com/archives/articles/2001/11/16/172201.shtml. See also Robert I. Friedman, "The Wobbly Israel Lobby; For the Once Potent AIPAC, It's Been a Very Bad Year," *Washington Post*, November 1, 1992.

28 Martin Peretz, "When America-Haters Become Americans," *New Republic*, October 15, 2001.

29 As reported in the *Los Angeles Times* by Solomon Moore in "Religion; Fiery Words, Disputed Meaning; Statements Made before September 11 Resurface in a Harsh New Light," November 3, 2002, B20.

30 News release, January 23, 2002.

31 Daniel Pipes, "Identifying Muslim Moderates," *Jewish World Review*, 25 November 25, 2003/30 Mar-Cheshvan, 5764, http://www.jewishworld review.com/1103/pipes_2003_11_25.php3.

32 The organizations to be condemned include Abu Sayyaf, Al-Gama'a al-Islamiyya, Groupe Islamique Armée, Hamas, Harakat ul-Mujahidin, Hizbullah, Islamic Jihad, Jaish-e-Mohammed, Lashkar-e-Tayyiba, and al-Qaeda. Pipes, "Identifying Muslim Moderates."

33 Pipes, "Identifying Muslim Moderates."

34 Pipes, "Identifying Muslim Moderates."

35 Pipes, "Identifying Muslim Moderates."

36 Daniel Pipes, "[Moderate] Voices of Islam," *New York Post*, September 23, 2003. http://www.danielpipes.org/1225/moderate-voices-of-islam.

37 Irshad Manji, *The Trouble with Islam: A Wake-Up Call for Honesty and Change* (Toronto: Random House Canada, 2003).

38 Eberhart, "Muslim Moderate Kabbani Firm."

39 These include the Islamic Supreme Council of America, the Council for Democracy and Tolerance, the American Islamic Congress, the Society for Humanity and Islam in America, the Ataturk Society, and the Assembly of Turkish American Associations. http://www.Jewishworldview.com/1103/pipes.

40 George W. Bush, "Presidential Address to the Nation," October 7, 2001, http://www.whitehouse.gov/news/releases/2001/10/2001.

41   Safi, *Progressive Muslims.*

42   Ralph Dannheisser, "Islam Compatible with Democracy, Not Monolithic, Muslim Panelists Say," U.S. Embassy Malaysia, http://usembassymalaysia .org.my/wf/wf0909_islam.html.

43   *In re Dow,* 213 Fed. 355, 357 (District Court, E.D. South Carolina, 1914), as cited by Moore, *Al-Mughtaribun,* 53; Khalil A. Bishara, *Origin of the Modern Syrian,* cited in Michael Suleiman, "Early Arab-Americans: The Search for Identity," in *Crossing the Waters,* ed. Hooglund, 44.

44   Samhan, "Politics and Exclusion," 14.

45   Samhan, "Politics and Exclusion," 11–28.

46   Samhan, "Politics and Exclusion," 16.

47   Amy K. Goott and Steven J. Rosen, eds., *The Campaign to Discredit Israel* (Washington, D.C.: American Israel Public Affairs Committee, 1983), 3–12.

48   Fischbach, "Government Pressures," 89.

49   *The New York Times,* May 25, 1973.

50   Samhan, "Politics and Exclusion," 26, emphasis in the original.

51   Areas designated as the Arab world by the State Department include the Middle East and North Africa.

52   Hamid Mowlana, George Gerbner, and Herbert I. Schiller, eds., *Triumph of the Image: The Media's War in the Persian Gulf—A Global Perspective* (Boulder, Colo.: Westview Press, 1992); Nicholas Berry, *Foreign Policy and the Press: An Analysis of The New York Times' Coverage of U.S. Foreign Policy* (New York: Greenwood Press, 1990); Kenneth I. Vaux, *Ethics and the Gulf War: Religion, Rhetoric, and Righteousness* (Boulder, Colo.: Westview Press, 1992).

53   Reeva S. Simon, *The Middle East in Crime Fiction: Mysteries, Spy Novels, and Thrillers from 1916 to the 1980s* (New York: Lilian Barber Press, 1989); Albert Hourani, *Western Attitudes towards Islam* (Southampton: Southampton University Press, 1974).

54   Linda Street, *Veils and Daggers: A Century of National Geographic's Representation of the Arab World* (Philadelphia: Temple University Press, 2000); Edmund Ghareeb, *Split Vision: The Portrayal of Arabs in the American Media* (Washington, D.C.: American-Arab Affairs Council, 1983); Janice J. Terry, *Mistaken Identity: Arab Stereotypes in Popular Writing* (Washington, D.C.: Arab-American Affairs Council, 1985).

55   Jack G. Shaheen, *Arab and Muslim Stereotyping in American Popular Culture* (Washington, D.C.: Center for Muslim-Christian Understanding, 1997); Shaheen, *Reel Bad Arabs: How Hollywood Vilifies a People* (New York: Olive Branch Press, 2001); Shaheen, *The TV Arab* (Bowling Green, Ohio: Popular Press, 1984).

Works Cited

◉

Abd-Allah, Umar Faruq. "Islam and the Cultural Imperative." Foundation Paper, Nawawi Foundation, Burr Ridge, Ill., 2004.

'Abd al-Rahman, 'A'isha. *Al-Isra'iliyyat fi al-Ghazu al-Fikri.* [Cairo], 1975.

Abduh, Muhammad. "Isti'anat al-Muslimin bi'l-Kuffar wa Ahl al-Bid'a wa al-Ahwa'." In 'Amara, *Al-A'mal al-Kamila li'l-Imam Muhammad 'Abdu.*

———. *Al-A'mal al-Kamila,* tahqiq wa-taqdim Mohammad 'Imarah. Cairo: Dar al-Shuruq, 1993.

Abdul-Rauf, Muhammad. "The Future of the Islamic Tradition in North America." In *The Muslim Community in North America,* edited by Earle H. Waugh, Baha Abu-Laban, and Regula B. Qureshi, 271–78. Edmonton: University of Alberta Press, 1983.

Abou El Fadl, Khaled. "Islamic Law and Muslim Minorities: The Juristic Discourse on Muslim Minorities From the Second/Eighth to the Eleventh/Seventeenth Centuries." *Islamic Law and Society* 1 (1994): 140–87.

———. "Striking a Balance: Islamic Legal Discourse on Muslim Minorities." In *Muslims on the Americanization Path?,* edited by Yvonne Yazbeck Haddad and John L. Esposito. New York: Oxford University Press, 2000.

Abraham, Nabeel. "Detroit's Yemeni Workers." *MERIP Reports* 53 (1977): 3–9.

————. "National and Local Politics: A Study of Political Conflict in the Yemeni Immigrant Community of Detroit, Michigan." Ph.D. diss., University of Michigan, 1978.

Adams, Charles J. "Mawdudi and the Islamic State." In Esposito, *Voices of Resurgent Islam*, 99–133.

Afzal, Omar. "Learn Not Copy: Movements Facing Challenges of the West." *Message*, March 1996.

Ahmad, Ayesha, and Neveen A. Salem. "Faiths Come Together at National Cathedral on National Day of Mourning." Islam On Line. Accessed January 31, 2004.

Ahmad, K., and Z. I. Ansari, eds. *Islamic Perspectives: Studies in Honour of Sayyid Abul A'la al-Mawdudi*. Leicester: Islamic Foundation, 1979.

Ahmad, Zaki. "Al-Ta'addudiyya al-Hizbiyya fi al-Fikr al-Islami al-Mu'asir." In *Nadwat al-Ta'addudiyya al-Hizbiyya*.

Ahmed, K., Arne Rudvin, et al. *Christian Mission and Islamic Da'wah: Proceedings of the Chambesy Dialogue Consultation*. Leicester: Islamic Foundation, 1982.

al-'Awwa, Muhammad Salim. *Fi al-Nizam al-Siyasi li al-Dawla al-Islamiya*. Cairo: Dar al-Shuruq, 1989.

al-Bahnasawi, Salim 'Ali. *Al-Ghazu al-Fikri li al-Tarikh wa al-Sira bayn al-Yamin wa al-Yasar*. Kuwait, 1985.

————. *Al-Hukm wa Qadiyyat Takfir al-Muslim*. Kuwait, 1985.

al-Faruqi, Ismail Raji. "Common Bases between the Two Religions in Regard to Convictions and Points of Agreement in the Spheres of Life." In *Seminar of the Islamic-Christian Dialogue*, 229–64. Tripoli: Republic Office of Foreign Relations, Socialist Peoples Libyan Arab Jamahiriya, 1981.

————. *Islam and Culture*. Kuala Lumpur: ABIM, 1980.

————. *Islam and Other Faiths*. Leicester: Islamic Foundation and International Institute of Islamic Thought, 1988.

————. *On Arabism: Urubah and Religion*. Amsterdam: Djambatan, 1962.

————. "The Role of Islam in Global Inter-Religious Dependence." In *Towards a Global Congress of the World's Religions*, edited by Warren Lewis, 19–38. Barrytown, N.Y.: Unification Theological Seminary, 1980.

————. *Tawhid: Its Implications for Thought and Life*. Kuala Lumpur: International Institute of Islamic Thought, 1982.

————. *Trialogue of the Abrahamic Faiths.* Herndon, Va.: International Institute of Islamic Thought, 1986.

al-Hudaybi, Hassan. *Du'at la Qudat.* Beirut, 1978.

al-Jindi, Anwar. *Afaq Jadadah fi al-Adab wa-al-Tarikh wa-al-Tarajum.* [Cairo]: Maktaat al-Anjulu al-Misriyah, [1978].

al-Marayati, Salam. "Formulating an Agenda of Political Actions for North American Muslims." In Muhammad Ahmadullah Siddiqui, *Islam.*

al-Qaradawi, Yusuf. *Al-Sahwa al-Islamiyya bayn al-Juhud wa al-Tatarruf.* Kitab al-Umma 4. Doha, Qatar, 1985.

————. *Ghayr al-Muslimin fi al-Mujtama' al-Islami.* Beirut, 1983.

————. *Zahirat al-Ghuluww fi al-Takfir.* Kuwait, 1985.

al-Qazzaz, Ayad. "The Arab Lobby: Toward an Arab-American Political Identity." *Al-Jadid* 3, no. 14 (1997).

————. "Images of the Arabs in American Social Science Textbooks." In *Arabs in America: Myths and Realities*, edited by Baha Abu Laban and Faith T. Zeadey, 113–31. Wilmette, Ill.: Medina University Press International, 1975.

al-Rashid, 'Abd al-Rahman. "Bay' al-I'lam al-'Arabi." *Al-Majalla*, no. 707 (August 14–20, 1994): 13.

al-Samirra'i, Nu'man 'Abd al-Raziq. *Al-Takfir: Judhuruh-Asbabuh-Mubarriratuh.* Jiddah, 1984.

al-Sawi, Salah. *Al-Ta'addudiyya al-Siyasiyya fi al-Islam.* Cairo, 1992.

al-Shuqayri, Ahmad. *al'-A'mal al-kamilah*; taqdim Anis Sayigh; tahrir Khayriyah Qasimiyah. Beirut: Markaz Dirasat al-Wahdah al-'Arabiyah, 2006.

'Amara, Muhammad, ed. *Al'-A'mal al-Kamila li'l-Imam Muhammad 'Abdu: al-Kitabat al-Siyasiyya.* Cairo: Al-Mu'assasa al-'Arabiyya li'l-Dirasat wa'l-Nashr, 1972.

————. "Al-Ta'addudiyya: al-Ru'ya al-Islamiyya wa al-Tahadiyat al-Gharbiyya." In *Nadwat al-Ta'addudiyya al-Hizbiyya*, 3–14.

An-Na'im, Abdullahi A. "Religious Minorities under Islamic Law and the Limits of Cultural Relativism." *Human Rights Quarterly* 9 (1987): 1–18.

Arab American Institute. "Demographics." Washington, D.C.: Arab American Institute, 2003. http://www.aaiusa.org/demographics.htm#Religion3.

Arkoun, Mohammed. *Al-Hawamil Wa-al-shawamil: hawl Al-Islam Al-mus'asir.* Beirut: Dar Al-Tali'ah, 2010.

Aswad, Barbara. *Arabic-Speaking Communities in American Cities.* New York: Center for Migration Studies, 1984.

'Atiyya, Muhyi al-Din. "Al-Ta'addudiyya: Qa'ima Biblioghrafiyya Intaqat." In *Nadwat al-Ta'addudiyya al-Hizbiyya.*

'Awad, Jabir Sa'id. "Mafhum al-Ta'addudiyya fi al-Adabiyyat al-Mu'asira: Muraja'a Naqdiyya." In *Nadwat al-Ta'addudiyya al-Hizbiyya.*

Bagby, Ihsan, Paul M. Pearl, and Bryan T. Froehle. "The Mosque in America: A National Portrait." Released by the Council on American-Islamic Relations, Washington, D.C., April 26, 2001.

Bakst, Jerome. "Arabvertising: The New Brand of Arab Propaganda." *Times of Israel,* April 1975, 15–23.

Bassiouni, M. C., ed. The Civil Rights of Arab-Americans: "The Special Measures." Information Paper 10. Belmont, Mass.: Association of Arab-American University Graduates, 1974.

Berman, Jerry J.. "A Public Policy Report." ACLU, Washington, D.C., October 10, 1982.

Berry, Nicholas. *Foreign Policy and the Press: An Analysis of The New York Times' Coverage of U.S. Foreign Policy.* New York: Greenwood Press, 1990.

Bush, George W. "Presidential Address to the Nation." October 7, 2001. The White House website. http://georgewbush-whitehouse.archives. gov/news/releases/2001/10/20011007-8.html.

———. "President's Remarks at National Day of Prayer." The White House website. http://georgewbush-whitehouse.archives.gov/news/ releases/2001/09/20010914-2.html.

———. "Remarks by the President at Islamic Center of Washington, D.C." The White House website. Accessed September 22, 2005. http://georgewbush-whitehouse.archives.gov/news/ releases/2001/09/20010917-11.html.

Cheng, Mae E. "Legal Catch-22 for Immigrants." *Newsday,* December 14, 2003.

Dahbany-Miraglia, Dina. "American Yemenite Jewish Interethnic Strategies." In *Persistence and Flexibility: Anthropological Perspectives on the American Jewish Experience,* edited by Walter B. Zenner, 63–78. Albany: State University of New York Press, 1988.

Daniel, Norman. *Islam and the West: The Making of an Image.* Oxford: One World, 1993.

Dannheisser, Ralph. "Islam Compatible with Democracy, Not Monolithic, Muslim Panelists Say." U.S. Embassy Malaysia. U.S.

Department of State website. http://usembassymalaysia.org.my/wf/wf0909_islam.html.

Djerejian, Edward P. "The United States and the Middle East in a Changing World: Diversity, Interaction and Common Aspirations." Policy paper delivered at Meridian House and at the Middle East Institute's 46th Annual Conference, October 16, 1992.

Eberhart, Dave. "Muslim Moderate Kabbani Firm on Terrorist Nuclear Threat." Newsmax.com, November 19, 2001. http://archive.newsmax.com/archives/articles/2001/11/16/172201.shtml.

El Fadl, Khalid Abou. *The Authoritative and the Authoritarian in Islamic Discourse: A Contemporary Case Study*. Dar Taiba, 1997.

————. "Islamic Law and Muslim Minorities: The Juristic Discourse on Muslim Minorities from the Second/Eighth to the Eleventh/Seventeenth Centuries." *Islamic Law and Society* 1, no. 2 (1994): 141–87.

————. *The Place of Tolerance in Islam*. Boston: Beacon Press, 2002.

————. "Striking a Balance: Islamic Legal Discourse on Muslim Minorities." In *Muslims on the Americanization Path?*, edited by Yvonne Yazbeck Haddad and John L. Esposito. New York: Oxford University Press, 2000.

Elkholy, Abdo A. *The Arab Moslems in the United States: Religion and Assimilation*. New Haven: College and University Press, 1966.

Emerson, Steven. *American Jihad: The Terrorists Living Among Us*. New York: The Free Press, 2002.

————. "The Other Fundamentalists." *New Republic*, June 12, 1995, 21–30.

Esack, Farid. *Qur'an, Liberation and Pluralism*. Oxford: One World, 1997.

Esposito, John L. "Ismail R. Al-Faruqi: Muslim Scholar-Activist." In *The Muslims of America*, edited by Yvonne Yazbeck Haddad. New York: Oxford University Press, 1991.

————, ed. *Voices of Resurgent Islam*. New York: Oxford University Press, 1983.

Faraj, Muhammad. *Al-Islam fi Mu'tarak al-Sira' al-Fikri al-Hadith*. Cairo, 1962.

Findley, Paul. *They Dare Speak Out: People and Institutions Confront Israel's Lobby*. Chicago: Lawrence Hill Books, 1989.

Fischbach, Michael R. "Government Pressure against Arabs in the United States." *Journal of Palestine Studies* 14, no. 3 (1985): 87–100.

Friedman, Robert I. "The Wobbly Israel Lobby; For the Once Potent

AIPAC, It's Been a Very Bad Year." *Washington Post*, November 1, 1992.

Ghareeb, Edmund. *Split Vision: The Portrayal of Arabs in the American Media*. Washington, D.C.: American-Arab Affairs Council, 1983.

Goott, Amy K., and Steven J. Rosen, eds. *The Campaign to Discredit Israel*. Washington, D.C.: American Israel Public Affairs Committee, 1983.

Griswald, William J. *The Image of the Middle East in Secondary School Textbooks*. New York: Middle East Studies Association of North America, 1975.

Haddad, Yvonne Yazbeck. "The Challenge of Muslim Minorityness: The American Experience." In *The Integration of Islam and Hinduism in Western Europe*, edited by W. A. R. Shadid and P. S. van Koningsveld, 134–53. Kampen: Kok Pharos, 1991.

———. "Christians in a Muslim State: The Current Egyptian Debate." In *Christian-Muslim Encounters*, edited by Yvonne Yazbeck Haddad and Wadi Zaidan Haddad, 381–98. Gainesville: University Press of Florida, 1995.

———. "Islamist Depictions of Christianity in the Twentieth Century." *Islam and Christian Muslim Relations* 11, no. 3 (2000): 75–94.

———. "The 'New Enemy'? Islam and Islamists after the Cold War." In *Altered States: A Reader in the New World Order*, edited by Phyllis Bennis and Michel Moushabeck, 83–94. New York: Olive Branch Press, 1993.

———. "The Qur'anic Justification for an Islamic Revolution." *Middle East Journal* 37, no. 1 (1982): 14–29.

———. "Sayyid Qutb: Ideologue of Islamic Revival." In Esposito, *Voices of Resurgent Islam*, 67–98.

Haddad, Yvonne Yazbeck, and Adair T. Lummis. *Islamic Values in the United States: A Comparative Study*. New York: Oxford University Press, 1987.

Hagopian, Elaine. "Minority Rights in a Nation State: The Nixon Administration's Campaign against Arab-Americans." *Journal of Palestine Studies* 5, nos. 1–2 (1975–1976): 97–114.

Hagopian, Elaine, and Ann Paden, eds. *The Arab-Americans: Studies in Assimilation*. Wilmette, Ill.: Medina University Press International, 1969.

Hamid, Muhammad 'Abd al-Hakim. *Zahirat al-Ghuluww fi al-Din fi al-'Asr al-Hadith*. Cairo, 1991.

Haney-López, Ian. *White by Law: The Legal Construction of Race*. New York: New York University Press, 1996.

Hassan, Hassan Muhammad. *Wasa'il Muqawamat al-Ghazu al-Fikri li-al-'Alam al-Islami*. Mecca, [1981].

"Has the Bush Administration Benefitted Muslim Americans?" *Minaret* 23, no. 5 (2001).

Hathout, Maher. "Islamic Work in North America: Challenges and Opportunities." In Muhammad Ahmadullah Siddiqui, *Islam*.

Hitti, Philip Khuri. *The Syrians in America*. New York: George H. Doran, 1924.

Hooglund, Eric J., ed. *Crossing the Waters: Arabic-Speaking Immigrants in the United States before 1940*. Washington, D.C.: Smithsonian Institution Press, 1987.

Hourani, Albert. *Western Attitudes towards Islam*. Southampton: Southampton University Press, 1974.

Huntington, Samuel P. "The Clash of Civilizations?" *Foreign Affairs* 72 (1993): 22–49.

Hussaini, Hatem I. "The Impact of the Arab-Israeli Conflict on Arab Communities in the United States." In *Settler Regimes in Africa and the Arab World: The Illusion of Endurance*, edited by Ibrahim Abu-Lughod and Baha Abu-Laban, 201–22. Wilmette, Ill.: Medina University Press International, 1974.

Huwaydi, Fahmi. *Li'l-Islam Dimuqratiyya*. Cairo, 1993.

———. *Muwatinun la Dhumiyyun: Mawqi' Ghayr al-Muslimin fi Mujtama' al-Muslimin*. Beirut, 1985.

Ibrahim, Sa'd al-Din. *Al-Ta'addudiyya al-Siyasiyya wa al-Dimuqratiyya fi al-Watan al-'Arabi*. Amman, 1989.

Jabara, Abdeen, "The FBI and the Civil Rights of Arab-Americans." *ADC Issues*, no. 5 (n.d.): 1.

Jackson, Sherman A. *Islam and the Black American: Looking toward the Third Resurrection*. New York: Oxford University Press, 2005.

———. "Islam(s) East and West: Pluralism between No-Frills and Designer Fundamentalism." In *September 11 in History: A Watershed Moment?*, edited by Mary L. Dudziak, 112–35. Durham: Duke University Press, 2003.

Jarisha, 'Ali Muhammad, and Muhammad Sharif al-Zaybaq. *Asalib al-Ghazu al-Fikri li-al-'Alam al-Islami*. Cairo, [1977].

Jarrar, Samir Ahmad. "Images of the Arabs in United States Secondary School Textbooks." Ph.D. diss., Florida State University, 1976.

Karim, Karim H. *Islamic Peril: Media and Global Violence.* Montreal: Black Rose Books, 2000.

Kassim, Husain. *Legitimizing Modernity in Islam: Muslim Modus Vivendi and Western Modernity.* Lewiston, Maine: Edwin Mellen Press, 2005.

Kettani, Muhammad Ali. *Muslim Minorities in the World Today.* London: Mansell, 1986.

Khan, M. A. Muqtedar. "Living on Borderlines: Beyond the Clash of Dialogue." In *Muslims' Place in the American Public Square,* edited by Zahid H. Bukhari, Sulayman S. Nyang, Mumtaz Ahmad, and John L. Esposito, 84–113. Walnut Creek, Calif.: AltaMira Press, 2004.

Kiernan, V. G. *The Lords of Human Kind: European Attitudes to the Outside World in the Imperial Age.* London: Pelican, 1972.

Kishk, Muhammad Jalal. *Al-Ghazu al-Fikri.* Cairo, 1975.

Kramer, Martin. "Islam vs. Democracy." *Commentary* 95, no. 1 (1993): 35–42.

Lattin, Don. "North American Muslims Ponder Effect of 9/11 on Them." *San Francisco Chronicle,* September 2, 2002, A3.

Madkur, Rajab. *Al-Takfir wa al-Hijra Wajhan li-Wajh.* Cairo, 1985.

Mahmud, 'Ali 'Abd al-Halim. *Al-Ghazu al-Fikri wa al-Tayyarat al-Mu'adiya li al-Islam.* Riyad, 1984.

———. *Al-Ghazu al-Fikri wa-Atharuhu fi al-Mujtama' al-Islami al-Mu'asir.* Kuwait, 1979.

Malek, Abbas. *News Media and Foreign Relations: A Multi-faceted Perspective.* Norwood, N.J.: Ablex, 1996.

Manji, Irshad. *The Trouble with Islam: A Wake-Up Call for Honesty and Change.* Toronto: Random House Canada, 2003.

Marr, Timothy Worthington. "Imagining Orientalism in America from the Puritans to Melville." Ph.D. diss., Yale University, 1997.

Mashhur, Mustafa. "Al-Ta'addudiyya al-Hizbiyya." *Al-Sha'b,* October 4, 1993.

Mehdi, Mohammad T. *Of Lions Chained: An Arab Looks at America.* San Francisco: New World Press, 1962.

———. *Peace in Palestine.* New York: New World Press, 1976.

———. *Terrorism: Why America Is the Target.* New York: New World Press, 1988.

Metcalf, Barbara Daly. "New Medinas: The Tablighi Jama'at in America and Europe." In *Making Muslim Space in North America and Europe,* edited by Barbara Daly Metcalf, 110–27. Berkeley: University of California Press, 1996.

Mokarzel, Salloum A. "Can We Retain Our Heritage? A Call to Form a Federation of Syrian Societies." *Syrian World* 3, no. 5 (1928): 36–40.

Moore, Kathleen. *Al-Mughtaribun: American Law and the Transformation of Muslim Life in the United States.* Albany: State University of New York Press, 1995.

Mowlana, Hamid, George Gerbner, and Herbert I. Schiller, eds. *Triumph of the Image: The Media's War in the Persian Gulf—A Global Perspective.* Boulder, Colo.: Westview Press, 1992.

Nadvi, Syed A. Hassan Ali. *Muslims in the West: The Message and Mission.* London: Islamic Foundation, 1983.

Nadwat al-Ta'addudiyya al-Hizbiyya wa al-Ta'ifiyya wa al-'Irqiyya fi al-'Alam al-'Arabi, 3–14. Herndon, Va.: International Institute of Islamic Thought, 1993.

Neff, Alixa. *Becoming American: The Early Arab Immigrant Experience.* Carbondale: Southern Illinois University Press, 1985.

Netanyahu, Binyamin. *Fighting Terrorism: How Democracies Can Defeat Domestic and International Terrorism.* New York: Farrar, Straus and Giroux, 1995.

————, ed. *International Terrorism, Challenge and Response: Proceedings of the Jerusalem Conference on International Terrorism.* New Brunswick, N.J.: Transaction Books, 1981.

————. *Terrorism: How the West Can Win.* New York: Farrar, Straus and Giroux, 1986.

Noor, Farish A. "The Other Malaysia: Panopticon Revisited." November 6, 2002, http://www.malaysiakini.com/columns/20634.

Nyang, Sulayman S. "Seeking the Religious Roots of Pluralism in the United States of America: An American Muslim Perspective." *Journal of Ecumenical Studies* 34, no. 3 (1997): 402–17.

Obeidat, Marwan M. "The Muslim East in American Literature: The Formation of an Image." Ph.D. diss., Indiana University, 1985.

Ong, Aihwa. "A Multitude of Spaces: Radical versus Moderate Islam." Paper presented at the AAA annual meeting in New Orleans, November 21, 2002.

Orfalea, Gregory. "Sifting the Ashes: Arab-American Activism during the 1982 Invasion of Lebanon." *Arab Studies Quarterly* 11, nos. 2–3 (1989): 207–26.

Osman, Mohamed Fathi. *The Children of Adam: An Islamic Perspective on*

Pluralism. Washington, D.C.: Center for Muslim-Christian Understanding, 1996.

————. "Towards a Vision and an Agenda for the Future of Muslim Ummah." In Muhammad Ahmadullah Siddiqui, *Islam*.

O'Sullivan, Jack. "If You Hate the West, Emigrate to a Muslim Country." *Guardian*, October 8, 2001, features pages, 4.

Palumbo, Michael. "Land without a People." 1987. http://mideastfacts. org/facts/index2.php?option=com_content&do_pdf=1&id=48.

Peretz, Martin. "When America-Haters Become Americans." *New Republic*, October 15, 2001.

Perlez, Jane. "Muslim-as-Apple-Pie Videos Are Greeted with Skepticism." *New York Times*, October 30, 2002.

Perry, Glenn. "Treatment of the Middle East in American High School Textbooks." *Journal of Palestine Studies* 4, no. 3 (1975): 46–58.

Pipes, Daniel. "Identifying Muslim Moderates." *Jewish World Review*, November 25, 2003/30 Mar-Cheshvan, 5764, http://www.jewishworldreview.com/1103/pipes_2003_11_25.php3.

————. "[Moderate] Voices of Islam." *New York Post*, September 23, 2003. http://www.danielpipes.org/1255/moderate-voices -of-islam.

————. "The Muslims Are Coming! The Muslims Are Coming!" *National Review*, November 19, 1990, 28–31.

Quraishi, M. Tareq. *Ismail al-Faruqi: An Enduring Legacy.* Plainfield, Ind.: Muslim Student Association, 1987.

Qutb, Sayyid. *Fi Zilal al-Qur'an.* 6 vols. Beirut, 1980.

————. *Milestones.* Indianapolis: American Trust, 1990.

Rahman, Fazlur. *Major Themes of the Qur'an.* Minneapolis: Bibliographica Islamica, 1980.

Ramadan, Tariq. *Western Muslims and the Future of Islam.* New York: Oxford University Press, 2003.

Sachedina, Abdulaziz. *The Islamic Roots of Democratic Pluralism.* New York: Oxford University Press, 2001), 139.

————. *The Qur'an on Religious Pluralism.* Occasional Paper Series. Washington, D.C.: Center for Muslim-Christian Understanding.

Saeed, Agha. "The American Muslim Paradox." In *Muslim Minorities in the West: Visible and Invisible,* edited by Yvonne Yazbeck Haddad and Jane I. Smith, 39–58. Walnut Creek, Calif.: AltaMira Press, 2002.

Safi, Omar. *Progressive Muslims: On Justice, Gender and Pluralism.* Oxford: One World, 2003.

Said, Edward. *Covering Islam: How the Media and the Experts Determine How We See the Rest of the World.* New York: Vantage Books, 1997.

Salman, 'Abd al-malik. "Al-Tasamuh Tijah al-Aqalliyyat Kadarura li al-Nahda." In *Nadwat al-Ta'addudiyya al-Hizbiyya.*

Samhan, Helen Hatab. "Politics and Exclusion: The Arab American Experience." *Journal of Palestine Studies* 16, no. 2 (1987): 11–28. http://www.jstor.org/stable/2537085.

Sephardic Archives. *The Spirit of Aleppo: Syrian Jewish Immigrant Life in New York, 1890–1939.* Brooklyn, N.Y.: Sephardic Community Center, 1986.

Shah, Mowahid. *The FBI and the Civil Rights of Arab-Americans.* Washington, D.C.: ADC Research Institute, 1986.

Shaheen, Jack G. *Abscam: Arabiaphobia in America.* Washington, D.C.: American-Arab Anti-Discrimination Committee, 1980.

———. *Arab and Muslim Stereotyping in American Popular Culture.* Washington, D.C.: Center for Muslim-Christian Understanding, 1997.

———. *Reel Bad Arabs: How Hollywood Vilifies a People.* New York: Olive Branch Press, 2001.

———. *The TV Arab.* Bowling Green, Ohio: Popular Press, 1984.

Siddiqui, Mona. "Islam: Issues of Political Authority and Pluralism." *Political Theology* 7, no. 3 (2006): 337–50.

Siddiqui, Muhammad Ahmadullah, ed. *Islam: A Contemporary Perspective.* Chicago: NAAMPS, 1994.

Siddiqui, Muzammil. "Unity and Diversity: Islamic Perspective." 1. Accessed June 3, 2007. http://www.theamericanmuslim.org/tam .php/features/articles/unity_and_diversity_islamic_perspective/.

Simmons, Gwendolyn Zoharah. "Are We Up to the Challenge? The Need for a Radical Reordering of the Discourse on Women." In Safi, *Progressive Muslims,* 233–48.

Simon, Reeva S. *The Middle East in Crime Fiction: Mysteries, Spy Novels, and Thrillers from 1916 to the 1980s.* New York: Lilian Barber Press, 1989.

Street, Linda. *Veils and Daggers: A Century of National Geographic's Representation of the Arab World.* Philadelphia: Temple University Press, 2000.

Suleiman, Michael. "Early Arab-Americans: The Search for Identity." In Hooglund, ed., *Crossing the Waters,* 37–54.

Taha, Mahmud Mohamed. *The Second Message of Islam.* Translated by Abdullahi A. An-Na'im. Syracuse: Syracuse University Press, 1987.

Terry, Janice J. *Mistaken Identity: Arab Stereotypes in Popular Writing.* Washington, D.C.: Arab-American Affairs Council, 1985.

Tolan, John V. *Saracens: Islam in the Medieval European Imagination.* New York: Columbia University Press, 2002.

U.S. Department of State. *Muslim Life in America.* Washington, D.C.: Office of International Information Programs, U.S. Department of State. http://infousa.state.gov/education/overview/muslimlife/demograp.htm; http://infousa.state.gov/education/overview/muslimlife/immigrat.htm.

Vaux, Kenneth I. *Ethics and the Gulf War: Religion, Rhetoric, and Righteousness.* Boulder, Colo.: Westview Press, 1992.

Wadud, Amina. "Alternative Qur'anic Interpretation and the Status of Women." In *Windows of Faith: Muslim Women Scholar-Activists in North America,* edited by Gisela Webb, 3–21. Syracuse: Syracuse University Press, 2000.

———. *Inside the Gender Jihad: Women's Reform in Islam.* London: One World, 2006.

Wolfowitz, Paul. Remarks at a Brookings Institution Issues Forum, September 5, 2002. http://www.brookings.edu/comm/events/20020905.pdf.

Young, Robert. *White Mythologies: Writing History and the West.* London: Routledge, 1990.

Zenner, Walter B. "The Syrian Jews of Brooklyn." In *A Community of Many Worlds: Arab Americans in New York City,* edited by Kathleen Benson and Philip M. Kayal, 156–69. Syracuse: Syracuse University Press, 2002.

Zikri, Wajih Abu. "A New American Religion for Muslims." *Al-Akhbar,* December 26, 2001. FIBIS-NES-2001-1226.